DUMBI MABIALA

Dirty Virgin

Embraced By The Father's Love

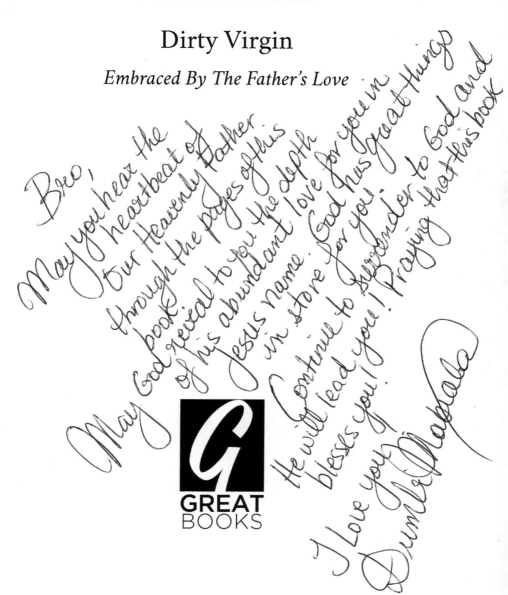

Bro,
May you hear the heartbeat of our Heavenly Father through the pages of this book. May God reveal to you the depth of his abundant love for you in Jesus name. God has great things in store for you. Continue to surrender to God and He will lead you! Praying that this book blesses you! I love you!

Dumbi Mabiala

GREAT BOOKS

"The Dirty Virgin" is a prophetic call to the Body of Christ to come back to the heart of God. Woven throughout this book is the love of God. Reading about the transformative power of God in this book is inspiring! Dumbi chose to take the pain and disappointment of life and exchange them for an eternal appointment with The King – Jesus. Dumbi poured out biblical truths that when applied, will set you free. As you read "The Dirty Virgin", you will hear the prophetic call to rise and take your place in Christ. You will hear the Father's call of love and purpose! You will hear the call to awaken as sons and daughters of God! This book is an inspiring read that will encourage, heal, and challenge you to walk in the transformation life of Christ.

Pastor Anthony and Pastor Gwendolyn Hill
PIR Ministries

Excellent page turner! Full of declarations, encouragement and hope for the Body of Christ. At first, I was leery about the title but as I carefully read each page, I found the title befitting. Dumbi's attention and intention to discuss her past shame, fears and insecurities is brave, but even more courageous is walking the reader towards God's redeemable and relentless love that He has for His children.

Pastor Nichole Brown
O.B.E.Y International Ministries

I find Dumbi to be a supremely relatable author and sister in Christ. Her vulnerable and transparent story of her own life journey through disappointment, abuse, delay, and ultimately, breakthrough is both inspiring and instructive. When it comes to what she believes and where she stands, Dumbi is unapologetic and authoritative (which is refreshing). Her work invites you as the reader to consider the formation of your spiritual identity across a continuum ranging from a sin mindset to a slave mindset to a sonship mindset. Along the way, she provides a clear framework for diagnosing where I am, where I've been, and where I'm going in the pursuit of a Christ-based identity which is both healthy and durable.

Pastor Phil Knauer
Echo Community Church

Obedience
Action
Consistency

First edition

Cover art by Roy Kamau
Editing by Megan McCoy
Back Cover Photo by Yasin Nkya

Contents

Introduction   iv
1 The Year of Laughter   1
2 No Longer an Orphan   21
3 The Bride Price   46
4 The Father's Heart   68
5 Identity of True Sons & Daughters   90
6 Created for Intimacy   120
7 Becoming Whole   136
8 Love Liberates   151
Conclusion   162
Notes   165
About the Author   166

Introduction

Our culture places very little value on the roles of fathers. From the way they are portrayed in mainstream culture to the lack of celebration of fatherhood, it seems that we've minimized their influence. Fathers are needed in our society. Their absence creates a significant void and negative consequences in our communities.

According to the U.S Census Bureau, an estimated 24.7 million children (33%) live absent of their biological fathers. The National Center for Fathering has determined that fatherlessness is the most significant family or social problem facing America. It's a real issue when our society witnesses more suicide taking place in fatherless homes or a higher increase of high school dropouts due to fathers' absence. There's no denying that fathers are needed in our society.[1]

Fathers or father figures, in many ways, prepare children to face life's challenges. They provide protection, confidence, safety, and stability. A father gives his family his name, which symbolizes identity, purpose, and a sense of belonging. As our Heavenly Father is the giver of life, so are our earthly fathers. They provide guidance and set the moral standards on how our families operate. Good, healthy fathers provide a value system that gives their families a proper foundation to excel in life.

Oftentimes, the climate in our homes and our upbringing determine the type of adults we will become in society. A healthy father in the home can make a significant difference to our communities. I understand that many people haven't experienced what it means to be fathered by a healthy and godly father. Some fathers are at home, but are not present nor involved in the lives of their children. I really believe that the enemy has been working to destroy families, to bring division, and to discredit good fathers. Fatherhood was God's idea for our society from the very beginning of creation in Genesis, but we know that Satan always perverts what God establishes.

Malachi 4:6 says, "And He will turn the hearts of the fathers to the children and the hearts of the children to their fathers."

In the very beginning, God instituted the idea of family. God's intention has always been for fathers to be the leaders of their households and to represent Him in the way they're called to love their families. His heart is to bring restoration to families and to turn fathers' hearts toward their children.

According to Dr. David Popenoe, Professor of Sociology at Rutgers University and Co-Director of the National Marriage Project, fathers are far more than just "second adults" in the home. *"Involved fathers—especially biological fathers—bring positive benefits to their children that no other person is as likely to bring. They provide protection and economic support and male role models. They have a parenting style that is significantly different from that of a mother and that difference is important in healthy child development."*[2]

In the same way, we need natural, healthy fathers in our homes; we also desperately need the embrace and direction of our Heavenly Father. As our culture is witnessing a breakdown in fatherhood, we're also seeing that manifested in the spiritual realm. There has been less of a reverence for God in the streets of our nations. I believe that the spirit of rebellion and division has entered our society and many are rejecting God's ideas and original intentions. God's plan has always been to partner with us as His sons and daughters. He's given us dominion that we may represent Him well in every aspect of society.

Satan's plan is to always discredit the character and Word of God. He knows that the moment we embrace and fully understand the gift of sonship and daughter-ship, we will become his biggest threat. Understand that Satan is not at war with God; he's too insignificant to be at war with our Heavenly Father. Satan is at war with us—God's children. He'll bring all manner of perversion and confusion to hinder us from fully walking in the delegated authority we have in Christ Jesus.

Additionally, there are some mindsets that we develop through life that stem from pain, trauma, or unprocessed disappointments. Those mindsets are contrary to our identity as sons and daughters of God. Part of maturing in God is yielding to His refining and purification process. As we dig deeper in the Word of God, it washes over us and begins to gently uproot thinking patterns that are not aligned with God's truth. All we need to do is continue to show up and avail ourselves to the Father who has the power to set us free from a life of bondage.

Nothing has the ability to disqualify you from experiencing the transforming power of the love of God, regardless of a past you may be ashamed of. God's intention has always been to do life with His children. It's the unconditional love of the father that confirms, affirms, and establishes us into our identity as a son or daughter of God and heirs to His eternal promise. When we allow the love of God to work within us, we will experience the fullness of His deliverance as we are set free from chains, unhealthy cycles, and mindsets that hold us captive.

You and I were not designed to live life as spiritual orphans, deprived of the place of security that our souls long for. When we live within the bounds of the Father's embrace, we no longer just exist, but we awaken to the significance of our calling as true spiritual sons and daughters. God's love is intentional and it desires to produce in us the likeness of Christ. The world around us, our families, and communities are eagerly expecting mature sons and daughters of God to authentically represent Christ in our generation. Through the pages of this book, experience an invitation to encounter the Father's heart and live the abundant life available to you as spiritual sons and daughters.

My prayer is that you will encounter the incomparable love of God that has the power to transform every area of your life. The Spirit of God relies on our willingness and availability to perform His eternal work in us.

1

The Year of Laughter

"Sometimes I laugh so hard that the tears run down my leg."
—Unknown

"Those who do not know how to weep with their whole heart don't know how to laugh either."
—Golda Meir

The year 2018 will go down in my personal history as one of the most challenging years of my life. It revealed deep-rooted wounds that were swept under my "Christian carpet." Unfortunately, every culture in our society has taboos. Certain topics are not encouraged to be mentioned. The Body of Christ is no different. The culture of the Body of Christ has allowed taboos to hide in the crevices of its house. I've sensed that God has been exposing our dirt for a while now, so He can cleanse our hearts. I believe that God always reveals to redeem.

God is ripping up the stinky old carpet and giving us significant makeovers. Scripture tells us in 1 Corinthians 6:19, that we're the temple of the Holy Spirit. We're God's dwelling place. God is invested in the transformation of His own house, which each of us represents. It's time to throw some things away and remodel God's house as He addresses patterns of thinking, mindsets, and religious practices that are contrary to His character.

It reminds me of the time, when Jesus was angry, that he made a whip of chords and flipped tables over as a way to cleanse the temple from all the merchant activities taking place there. He drove away all those vendors and scattered the coins of money changers because he wanted people to understand that His Father's house was not a place of commerce (see John 2:13–16). God is really serious about purging His bride (you & I). If we're going to be the church that Jesus is coming back for, we need to allow God to clean His house. We need to yield to the perfecting work of the Holy Spirit in our lives.

God's love for each of us is so fierce and unrelenting that it constantly pursues us. That's why God is more committed to our transformation than we are. He does the beautiful work in us as we yield. After all, the Bible tells us that we are God's masterpiece. We're the clay that's being worked on.

The Master Potter is intricately and meticulously perfecting us into His likeness. The challenge is sometimes it takes us forever to come to a place of total surrender so we can be molded into God's design. It's interesting that when a potter prepares the clay, sometimes he will use a method called spiral wedging.

Spiral wedging is a method used to roll the clay in a spiral motion for the purpose of removing impurities and any air bubbles to make the clay more consistent. The next step is the process of centering the clay on the wheel and creating the proper form. If these steps are not properly executed through the various stages, air bubbles can cause issues if they remain in the clay during firing. They can potentially cause the clay body to break and sometimes explode. In the same way, God's plan is to remove contaminants from our clay body as He works through the molding, massaging, and purification process. When we yield to God's ways, we won't break under fire.

There are a lot of things happening in the Body of Christ that God is shining a light on. We often choose not to bring those subjects up because sometimes it's uncomfortable to talk about. As you read through the pages of this book, you'll notice that I'm a transparent person, and I often don't shy away from discussing real issues. Additionally, as an introvert, I hate small talk. So, let's get to the real stuff! You'll understand that my purpose in speaking about certain topics in this book is not only to share my story but to also highlight God's redemptive nature.

Stay with me and you'll see why I titled this chapter, *The Year of Laughter*.

Do me a favor though, make yourself comfortable, grab yourself a cup of coffee or tea (or any beverage of your choice), and let's get on this beautiful journey.

Let's pull back the curtains and candidly talk about some of these interesting topics.

Taboo #1

Spiritual abuse is one of the taboos I barely hear anyone talk about. I don't think I've ever heard a podcast or message discussing how to heal from it. But it's real. We don't talk about the pain that countless people suffer in the hands of tyrannic and unloving spiritual leaders who abuse their authority through their words and actions. It's so sad that these individuals claim to represent Christ but really don't. I applaud and recognize that there is great Kingdom leadership out there in our society, but let's also acknowledge that not everyone is a good leader. Folks have been brainwashed by so-called leaders who were hungry for power and control. A lot of churches, unfortunately, have allowed the spirit of Jezebel and other demonic spirits to sit on the throne and lead their congregations through manipulation, fear, and control. It's evident there's something wrong when a church leader declares that a member will become sick, poor, will totally miss their calling if they leave their church, or when a leader blatantly tells you that you can't make any life decisions without running everything through them.

I'm not telling you something that I haven't experienced. I've lived through it. I've been a victim of spiritual abuse for years in the hands of leaders, who obviously did not have the heart of the Father, so-called "leaders," who manipulated people's vulnerability and naivety. There are tons of leaders out there in the church, who are intimidated by the gift that their members carry, and as a result, they stifle and restrain people's growth. Some have falsely prophesied into people's lives and given directions that were not in agreement with God's counsel. Those are the leaders who refuse to have mentors who can keep them accountable. As a result, they created unhealthy cultures in the church that glorified them and promoted false teachings, therefore, leading many away from the truth of God's word.

At that time, the traumatic experience I went through distorted my understanding of our Heavenly Father in some ways. I had a misguided perception of God's image as a result of the leaders in my life who had misrepresented Him. God, in His mercy, took me out of that destructive environment I was in. It took me a fairly long time to be spiritually, emotionally, and mentally healthy again. I didn't want to be a part of the statistics of people who experienced church hurt and quit serving God as a result of it. I knew I had to take the necessary time to heal and separate the painful experiences I had from my personal encounters with who I knew God to be. God was still a very faithful Father. He was still a good God in spite of my circumstances and the emotional and spiritual abuse I had endured. God wasn't responsible for these evil deeds and the way that people choose to behave.

I love the Church and the people of God. I love to serve His Body. I love how God pours out His Spirit on us, leads us, walks with us, speaks to us, and lavishes His passion over us. It's amazing to me that God is madly in love with us. I believe in Kingdom leadership when people carry true compassion, justice, integrity, and the heart of Jesus into everything they do. That's the Body of Christ that I'm a part of. A Church Body that honors God, edifies one another, and works together in advancing the Kingdom of God -not one that is greedy for power and in love with the spirit of mammon. God is doing remarkable work in His house, raising giants after His kind, and sitting down wolves in sheep's clothing who have no business leading the flock.

Taboo #2

Chronic Depression is another taboo that plagues the people of God but is also rarely talked about in Christian circles. Albeit, I'm very encouraged because I've been hearing a lot more conversations about mental health in recent years. People are a lot more open these days to having these types of conversations in the church. I came from a cultural background that doesn't necessarily encourage folks to pursue medical help to address their mental needs.

Growing up, I would hear many people say, *"just pray about it, and you'll be fine."* Trust me, I deeply believe in the power of prayer and its benefits, but I'm also aware that we are spirit, soul, and body. There are some psychological and physiological needs that we have that may require practical or medical solutions. I've come to understand that people can be highly effective, driven, and functional, but yet constantly overwhelmed with deep sadness and hopelessness. This is not the occasional bad day that many of us have experienced; it's deeper than that, and I truly believe that our approach to handling mental illness should involve both spiritual and medical remedies.

It utterly grieves my heart when I hear of leaders who take their lives due to years of struggle with depression. This battle is real and we need to continue to talk about it so more people can be given the spiritual, natural, and health remedies to combat it. No doubt that there are natural causes that predispose someone to experience depression-like chemical or hormonal imbalance, or undealt childhood trauma, but there are also some spiritual implications that we do not want to ignore. I wholeheartedly believe that a lot of circumstances that we deal with in the natural world have been conceived in spiritual or demonic realms.

Don't misquote me. I'm of the belief that you can love Jesus with your entire being and still see a therapist to work through mental illness. The same way when you have the flu, you ask for God's healing power to touch your body, and at the same time, you go to the doctor to get a prescription to address the symptoms so you can be healed. We need to have both natural and spiritual remedies to combat this because destinies are being cut short.

If you are in any emotional distress or feeling suicidal, please call the National Suicide Prevention Lifeline at 1-800-273-8255 to speak to a counselor who can help you.

In 2018, there were moments when I was depressed and suicidal. I knew that I was engaged in deep spiritual warfare. It felt like all hell broke loose, and that everything I had built in life up to that point was crumbling. My professional life was in shambles as I had just been laid off from a good job that I had been at for several years. My romantic life was non-existent at the time, as I was trying to make sense of the countless failed relationships I've had. Add to the turmoil some personal and family issues I was navigating at the time.

Life is interesting, isn't it? It's full of ups, downs, turns, valleys, and mountains. We've all experienced seasons in our lives when we feel that life has been pouring down heavy rain for a long time. Do you know what I'm talking about? That moment when the wind disrespectfully blows your umbrella away. You're left completely uncovered, with no sense of security. Then, you sit on the side of the road completely drenched and wonder what your next step should be. When life happens, it happens with vengeance.

The level of disappointment in my life was absurd. It made absolutely no sense. I couldn't understand how someone who had served God passionately for the past fifteen years, could find herself in such a low state. My mind became a playground where the enemy was ferociously bombarding me with his lies. I was mentally exhausted from the constant exercise of having to tear down thoughts that were originating right from the pit of hell. I can truthfully say that God kept me. God's truth sustained me as I was going through that difficult season. His word was my anchor.

To be honest, I didn't always have the strength to open the Bible, but when I did, it was my lifeline. The few friends who knew I was going through this challenge kept me in prayer and were always checking on me. My family was my rock as they've always been; their constant love supplied the hope I needed. What I believe made a significant impact in my life during that difficult season was that I immersed myself in deep worship. Anointed worship songs would be playing in my ears day and night, and I would actually sleep with worship music playing throughout the night. I saturated my soul with thoughts of God that reminded me daily of His love. God's love indeed kept me alive.

It Was Necessary!

Hindsight is always 20/20. Looking back at my life, I can sincerely say that I'm grateful for the year that broke me. Well, obviously if I had the option though, I would have totally avoided most of life's painful events. However, I know that without experiencing the breakdown, I would have never stopped long enough to realize that I desperately needed healing in my soul. I wouldn't have known that I was just going through the motions and living my Christian life on cruise control. The breaking is sometimes necessary because it reveals the wounds and hurt we need to heal from. I think the breaking is a blessing in disguise. Sometimes our biggest breakthroughs in life come after our biggest breakdowns.

In a way, a hard year or unforeseen circumstances can stop you in your tracks so you can focus inwardly and assess your life. If we can all be honest, the year 2020 provided that for many of us. I don't think anyone was prepared to navigate life in the midst of a global pandemic, and I'm sure most of us would have wanted to flush 2020 down the toilet and get a do-over (raise both of your hands if you agree with me).

The global pandemic of 2020 revealed our deepest fears, sorrows, doubts, brokenness, loneliness, and frailties. In many ways, it gave us a 20/20 vision. It allowed us to see what was important and what was not; it also highlighted our desperate need for God. Our culture may still deny it, but the truth remains that we need God's presence to invade every aspect of our society. From our government to our educational system, our family dynamics, or the judicial system, the soul of every human being cries out for intimacy with God.

We can't go through life hiding behind the banner of being called a child of God and yet ignoring the state of our souls (mind, will, and emotions). We live in a society that is always on the move and we don't stop long enough to examine the condition of our spiritual, mental, or emotional well-being. We are encouraged by the medical community to schedule a physical examination at the beginning of each year to go through our check-ups and blood work to ensure that we have a clean bill of health, yet we rarely take the same approach in regards to our mental, emotional, or spiritual health.

When was the last time you stopped long enough to think about how you're really doing? It often takes drastic life events to slow us down so God can reveal what we need to attend to. We cannot pretend that those areas we choose not to deal with are not corroding our souls. I believe that God desires for us to be whole-completely whole. It's possible that our thought-life can be pure and healthy even as we live in a culture that promotes all manner of perversion. Our emotions can be rooted and grounded in God's truth. We can live a thriving spiritual life as we continue to seek God in all we do. A healthy life is attainable. We don't have to live in dysfunction when an abundant life is available to each of us.

"This Is My Year"

When I look back at the beginning of 2018, I was filled with so much hope and joy at the anticipation of what I thought could be one of my best years yet. In January of 2018, I hosted a communication and speaking seminar to empower leaders who desired to increase their influence and ability to connect more effectively with others. It was quite a successful event from the feedback that I received and the quality relationships that were birthed from that event.

It was an exceptional way to kick off the year. The sense of accomplishment and significance left me believing that 2018 was the year to see my dreams fulfilled. The success I longed for in my career and personal life seemed to be a finger-tip length away. I had a deep sense that it was going to be a defining year in my life professionally and romantically, and it surely was, but not in the way that I envisioned. I was completely done with the years of drought, tears, and struggle. I was sick and tired of being sick and tired. I was eager to do what it takes to break the cycle of setbacks in my life. I was ready for change, ready to pursue my dreams, and to fully embrace the woman God had called me to be, but little did I know that life had a series of unpleasant surprises waiting for me as a bully waits for his victim at the back of the school. I sure wasn't ready for the punches that life threw at me, because they almost knocked me out of the race.

When Life Doesn't Look Like The Promise

Like some of you, I start every new year seeking God for guidance and wisdom. I spend some time asking God to reveal His will for my life. I also posture my heart to yield to God's plans for that particular year, so I typically begin my year with a word from the Lord. In the past, God has been really faithful to give me a prophetic word that would provide direction and focus for my entire year.

That year, God spoke to me through a friend during a conversation we had. My friend strongly felt in her heart that 2018 was going to be the year of laughter for me. I was ecstatic to receive that word, and it resonated in my heart. I decided to run with that word. 2018 indeed was going to be the year of laughter. That was my declaration. Given that the prior years of my life have been filled with so many tears and deep sadness, I was ready to experience a season of laughter.

Until that point in my life, I felt like the woman with the issue of blood in Luke 8:43-48. The Scriptures talk about a woman who had suffered from bleeding for twelve years. Twelve whole years! That's a very long time to deal with any kind of problem. She spent her life's wages seeking doctors' help, but no one could help her. She was socially outcast and ashamed of her condition, but I imagine that she still held on to hope.

> *"And a woman who had suffered from a flow of blood for twelve years and had spent all her living upon physicians, and could not be healed by anyone, came up behind Him and touched the fringe of His garment, and immediately her flow of blood ceased." Luke 8:43-45 (AMPC)*

Some of us have endured chronic conditions in life that have left us emotionally, spiritually, or even financially bankrupt. At times, we're hemorrhaging and don't even realize that we've been bleeding for a while, but when we come to the awareness of our brokenness and the pain of our situation, we become desperate for healing. The woman with the issue of blood desperately needed a touch from Jesus. She worked her way through the crowd and touched the fringe of his garment. Twelve years of pain, shame, and agony were healed in a moment of faith. That's where I was in my life. Totally desperate for an encounter with Jesus. I was convinced that the year of laughter would usher in the encounter I desperately needed. I was hopeful that at last, my heart's desires would come to fruition.

During that season, the Scripture that the Holy Spirit highlighted to me was the story of Abraham and Sarah. In the story of Abraham and Sarah, God first spoke to Abraham (then Abram) and gave him the promise of a child when he was about 75 years old. God made a covenant with Abraham that an heir will be born from him; that he will have many descendants and be a great nation.

Put yourself in Abraham's sandals for a moment, as we explore this thought. I'm pretty sure that he thought God's promise would likely be fulfilled within a year or maybe two. Don't you love it when God gives you a promise but doesn't give you the tracking number to monitor the package? Why don't you tell me when I'm supposed to expect the package to arrive?

God will give you a word but doesn't tell you when it's supposed to come to pass. It's funny when God says soon—it could be anywhere between two to five years. *Can I get an amen somebody?* I get it. There would be no need for faith if we knew all the details of our lives.

Anyways, let's get back to the story.

Ten years after God spoke to Abraham, there was still no evidence of a

THE YEAR OF LAUGHTER

child, so Sarai (she wasn't called Sarah yet) decided to be creative. She felt it would be a good idea for Abraham to sleep with their maidservant, Hagar, because she didn't see how she could conceive a child in her old age.

Let's think about this situation from Sarai's perspective now. Here she is, definitely a senior citizen when God first mentioned the promise of a child. At this point, she's postmenopausal. Her ovaries definitely stopped producing hormones and her eggs have dried up a long time ago. I'm sure she's thinking that Abraham will probably need a heavy dosage of Viagra to even reach an erection. What used to be a simple intimate act will now require a resurrection. And besides, how can an old and tired body like hers carry a pregnancy for nine whole months?

It's interesting to me that sometimes we read these Bible stories and completely dismiss that these people had real human concerns. They looked at their situations and didn't always see how God's word was going to be fulfilled. We've all been there, haven't we? In that strange place of disconnect when your current reality doesn't match what God promised. It's a tough place to be for many of us if we're honest. Unfortunately, it's in that place between living by faith or unbelief that we choose to make decisions that are often contrary to God's plans.

Almost twenty-five years later from the first time God spoke to Abraham about having an heir, that God visited Abraham again. God spoke to Abraham and Sarai to reinforce the word that He had previously given them about bearing a child. Abraham laughed. Who knows, he probably laughed in unbelief at this point. Let's look at Genesis 17.

> "And God said to Abraham, As for Sarai your wife, you shall not call her name Sarai; but Sarah [Princess] her name shall be.
>
> And **I will bless her and give you a son also by her.** Yes, I will bless her, and she shall be a **mother of nations**; Kings of peoples shall come from her.
>
> Then Abraham fell on his face and **laughed** and said in his heart, shall a child be born to a man who is a hundred years old? And shall Sarah,

who is ninety years old, bear a son?

And [he] said to God, Oh, that Ishmael might live before You!

*But God said, **Sarah your wife shall bear you a son indeed,** and **you shall call his name Isaac [laughter];** and I will establish My covenant or solemn pledge with him for an everlasting covenant and with his posterity after him." Gen 17:15-19 AMPC*

Abraham had to push back any feeling of doubt and unbelief as the word of the Lord came to Him again. He had something to hold on to. We know how the rest of the story unfolds. God kept His promise and Abraham and Sarah received their promised child. How amazing that God told Abraham to name Isaac *"laughter"* or translated literally as *"he laughs."* Every time Abraham would call his son's name, I'm sure he was reminded that God got the last laugh. Isn't that ironic? God indeed keeps His promises.

Just like Abraham, I held on to the prophetic word and promises that God gave me. This was going to be my year of laughter and rejoicing. I believed that I was coming to the end of a painful journey, a journey of suffering and spiritual opposition. Up to that point in my life, many of the prophetic words that I received were about spiritual warfare being fierce and the enemy constantly opposing my life. I was tired of hearing that. I just wanted a simple life with no drama or foolishness. After all, I told God that I'd never raised my hand for the life He called me to. I didn't volunteer for this, and as an intercessor, I knew that I needed some encouragement.

I needed a time of refreshing and a time to heal my broken soul. As a soldier in the army of the Lord, I felt as if I had been in the trenches for a very long time standing in the gap for my family, friends, my community, and my church. I was emotionally and spiritually weary. I was totally burned out. I needed a break, but most of all I needed an encounter. I knew in that season that I desperately needed my Heavenly Father's embrace.

Generally speaking, I've always been a very happy person in life. I tend to naturally look at life from a positive angle. The cup is always half-full in my mind. I'm not one to complain a lot regarding personal things I go through. I tend to believe that I have a pretty high tolerance for pain. However, I've come to understand that there's only so much that a soldier can endure. I knew I was wounded, and I needed God to nurse me back to life.

I've experienced deep betrayal from really close friends. I have experienced injustices in the workplace on many occasions. I've been judged and accused of things I've never said or done. I've been spiritually and emotionally abused by people who are supposed to look out for me. In a nutshell, I've been deeply wounded by life events like many of you. This journey is not about me vomiting the unfortunate circumstances that I experienced in life in the hope to get your sympathy. Nope. My desire is to take you with me on this journey of growth and discovery, so we can both come to a deeper revelation of the love of The Father. I've learned that all things - the good, the bad, and the ugly - work together for good, for those who love God and who are called according to His purpose (Romans 8:28).

The Scripture does not say that everything that happens to us is good - of course not. We could paraphrase that Scripture by saying that God's plan is to bring the good out of every situation we go through including the painful ones. The Word of God reminds us that it rains on the just and unjust alike. The truth is, bad things happen to good people too. We live in a fallen world and people sometimes make bad decisions that negatively affect the lives of others.

There is one Bible character I've always identified with most of my Christian walk. He was a dreamer, chosen by God with a great call on his life. I'm referring to Joseph (his story is told in the book of Genesis 37-50). Most of us know his story of pain, betrayal by his brothers, being sold into slavery, and being falsely accused of things he did not do.

Certainly, it wasn't fun being Joseph in the early years of his life. How do you go from pain to calamity and still love God with the same fervency? How can you be sold into slavery by your own brothers and believe that good could still come out of it? I don't necessarily know the mental and spiritual roller coaster that Joseph endured through his difficulties, but we can at least gather that his faith in God never wavered. Regardless of the opposition, the hardship, or the shame he endured, Joseph still persisted. He wasn't bitter about life's disappointments.

I didn't realize that the years of undealt disappointments in my life opened the door to unbelief and bitterness. I was unaware that my heart had grown numb towards the nudges of the Holy Spirit. I wasn't stepping out in faith as I used to. I was risk-averse and afraid to believe again.

I didn't recognize the person I had become. My passion for the Lord was slowly dwindling, yet I was still in ministry, serving others and believing that God would bless their socks off.

For some reason, It was easier to believe for other people. It was easier to stand in the gap for others and ignore the deep pain I was going through. How did this happen to me? I had served God since I was 18 years old; I was now in my early 30's and I was struggling in my faith. I've always been that young lady on fire for the Lord and passionate about advancing His Kingdom.

What I was dealing with was years of unprocessed disappointments but I couldn't put a finger on it at the time.

Navigating Through Disappointment

Let's look at the origin of the word disappointment to better understand what the word means. According to the online etymology dictionary, the word disappoint has a french origin and it essentially means to fail to keep an appointment.

Dis-appoint: 'dis' means reverse, opposite of appoint. It means to undo the appointment. In a modern sense, it means "to frustrate the expectation or desires of" or "defeat the realization or fulfillment of a thing."

In contrast, the word "appoint" means "to resolve", "to settle" and "to arrange the time of a thing."

So when we're dis-appointed, it means that our expectation was cut short. It reveals unmet expectations and desires that were not fulfilled. Scripture tells us in Proverbs 15:13 that sorrow of the heart breaks the spirit. In other words, when your heart is in pain, it weakens your spirit. That's why we have to learn to process pain and emotions because it negatively affects our spirits, but learning to overcome disappointment is no small task. It's a process we all need to navigate in life. We can all agree that disappointment is one of those unwelcomed guests in our lives that we wish we could live without.

The truth is that disappointment is inevitable. It's part of life. However, unprocessed disappointments can be very detrimental to our souls. When we've been hit several times in life and don't take time to heal, it's often hard to move forward. When people are in that space, many feel stuck. It's hard to see the path forward when you're consumed with your disappointment. Most often when we've been hurt, we tend to focus inwardly, and therefore, our disappointment is magnified. The danger in unprocessed disappointment is to camp there and filter all of your life experiences through that distorted lens.

What have you been hoping for that hasn't come to fruition yet? Is it the new entrepreneurial journey you were excited about that fell through? Or maybe you were hoping you would be married by now. Or perhaps you were hoping you would be further in your career or be qualified for the house of your dreams.

Sometimes the disappointment in our lives blinds us from experiencing the presence of God. The key to overcoming disappointment is to acknowledge the presence of Jesus in the midst of the disappointment. When you have knowledge that God is with you in the process, it gives you peace to better navigate those challenging storms.

Undealt disappointment will hinder you from trusting, loving, taking risks, and moving forward in life.

The key to overcoming disappointment is to acknowledge the presence of Jesus in the midst of the disappointment.

How Do We Overcome Disappointment?

By now, you can probably tell that I'm a big fan of Abraham's story. Let's dive into Romans 4:

> "*[For Abraham, human reason for] hope being gone, **hoped in faith** that he should become the father of many nations, as he had been promised, So [numberless] shall your descendants be.*
>
> ***He did not weaken in faith** when he considered the [utter] impotence of his own body, which was as good as dead because he was about a hundred years old, or [when he considered] the barrenness of Sarah's [deadened] womb.*
>
> *No unbelief or distrust made him waver (doubtingly question) concerning the promise of God, but **he grew strong and was empowered by faith** as he gave praise and glory to God, **fully satisfied and assured that God was able and mighty to keep His word and to do what He had promised.**" Romans 4:18-21 (AMPC)*

Abraham had hope, not just faith. His faith was the proof of confident hope. **If faith is a car, hope is the fuel that keeps it running.** Against the possibility of anything coming to fruition, Abraham still believed. He believed that he would be the father of many nations as God promised. Despite his old age and the incapacity of his reproductive organs, Abraham believed that God's ability to perform His word wasn't limited by his circumstances. This hope that Abraham stood on wasn't mere optimism. It was backed by the consistency of God's character. God cannot lie. It's never been His nature nor His character.

If faith is a car, hope is the fuel that keeps it running.

What God spoke over your life will come to pass. If God said it, It will happen regardless of the delay or opposition in your life. Friend, I know that you are still waiting on the fulfillment of many promises, but be encouraged. God can be trusted. Hold on to hope just like Abraham and the woman with the issue of blood did. Hope is the earnest expectation that God will do what he promised at the right time and in the right way. Hope is that unwavering attitude that God's word will come to pass.

I believe that hope is the antidote to disappointment. It's a deep-rooted belief that is anchored in Jesus. **In the absence of any justification for hope, Abraham still believed.** Take a moment here to replace your name, where Abraham's name is underlined. Let's read that sentence again.

In the absence of any justification for hope, _____ still believed. Powerful, isn't it?

If hope is the remedy against disappointment, the question is: *"How do I grow in hope?" I'm glad you asked.*

You grow in hope by saturating your mind, heart, and emotions with the truth of God's word. Hope has a name. His name is Jesus. You grow in hope by intentionally deciding not to be negative in your thinking. You grow in hope by speaking God's thoughts over your life and over the situations you're still believing for. You grow in hope by choosing not to live in fear and taking these small faith-filled steps.

Hope can sometimes feel like a torn bulletproof vest in a world that is bombarded with so much negativity and calamity, but the good news is that it doesn't matter how many bullets hit that vest, it can always be refurbished.

Your hope can be renewed. One of the ways to do that is to expose the disappointment and invite the presence of Jesus into your pain. God is big enough to handle your disappointment and raw emotions. God knows you inside and out. He knows the depth of your thoughts and is so aware of the intentions of your hearts. It's OK to be vulnerable with God and tell him how you really feel about the situation or the lost opportunity.

Key Steps To Take To Heal From Disappointment:

- Acknowledge the disappointment.

- Allow yourself to feel every emotion - don't suppress it (anger, sadness, apathy, etc.).
- Invite Jesus into those painful areas.
- Ask God to open your eyes so you can recognize His presence with you.
- Take time to grieve - cry if you need to.
- Let go and decide that you will not hold on to disappointment.
- Get a fresh vision from God concerning your present and future.
- Decide to move forward no matter what.

God Will Get The Last Laugh - Hold On To His Promises

The year of laughter revealed that my heart was similar to Sarah's—a disappointed heart—caught between unbelief and faith, unsure if God's promises would ever come to fruition. Like Sarah, we become impatient when we deem that God is taking too long to do what he has promised us, so we come up with our own ideas to "help" God. We forget that we will have to live with the consequences of acting on ideas that were never part of God's original plan. When God made a covenant with Abraham and promised him that he would be the father of many nations. The fulfillment of that word was to come through Isaac - the promised seed.

As we discussed earlier in the chapter, Sarah thought it would be clever that Abraham would sleep with Hagar to secure that seed, and that's how Abraham's firstborn, Ishmael, made his entrance into the world. When we look at history, we understand that Ishmael is considered to be the ancestor of the Arabic nations. Isaac, on the other hand, was the heir God chose to carry out Abraham's legacy and to bring redemption to the Jewish nation.

We often deceive ourselves when we think that we can take matters into our own hands and somehow expedite the package we're expecting God to deliver. In the story of Abraham, Sarah, and Hagar, we see how one night of disobedience can produce a lifetime of discord between nations. To this day, the Jews and the Arabs have enmity towards each other because of issues that originated from Abraham's household.

Abraham and Sarah's disobedience didn't just alter the course of history, but it also propagated fatherlessness in the land. God told Abraham that through his seed, he would be the father of many nations. This indicates that the concept of fatherhood was very important to God. When Hagar and Ishmael were asked to leave Abraham's household, it introduced the spirits of rejection, abandonment, and fatherlessness into the mix. Imagine what a fifteen-year-old Ishmael felt when he was forced to leave his father's house? He must have felt like an outcast, and I believe that same spirit of rejection was translated into the Muslim religion.

In the Muslim faith, Ishmael is recognized as the patriarch of their faith and an ancestor to Muhammad (the founder of Islam). It is said that Muslims do not see God as a father figure. The notion of intimate friendship and relationship with God is non-existent in the Muslim faith. In fact, in the Quran, there are 99 names for God, but none mean "Father." I once ministered to a Muslim woman who was offended when I addressed God as my Heavenly Father. I recall she was perturbed that I would describe God as my Father. She kept on saying to me that God is not my Father and that He's simply God.

This faulty doctrine that many believe in is sadly the proof that Satan perverts everything that God designs. God's intention has always been to father His children. Jesus' relationship with God, The Father, serves as a prototype of what is also available to us. Everything that Jesus did was to demonstrate what was possible when we put our faith in Him. From the miracles He performed to His closeness with our Heavenly Father, Jesus is the forerunner we should seek to imitate. The Father and Jesus are one, so we could also be one with Him.

If you've ever found yourself like Sarah, weary and tired of declaring God's promises over your life, trust me, I get it. I've been standing on the Word of God and speaking it over various areas of my life for years. Decades have passed, and I'm still waiting. And if I can be 100 percent honest with you, my friend, I get frustrated as well. As I'm writing this book on a sunny, Saturday afternoon, I wonder when the wait will finally be over. I still have no clue of the journey ahead, but I choose every day to trust God. I know there's gotta be purpose in the wait. Resilience is forged as we wait on God's promises. Some days are better than others. Other days, my faith is limping, but I refuse to give up. God knows the plans that He has for each of us, and we have to trust His timing.

In due time, He will surely perfect everything concerning us.

I can tell you one thing—I'm committed to march according to God's divine orders no matter what comes my way. The safest place to be on this planet is in the perfect will of our Heavenly Father. I can say with assurance that I believe that God will get the last laugh in my life.

Friend, I'd like to encourage you to strengthen your tired hands and weakened knees. This is not the time to throw in the towel. When you've done all you know to do, remain standing. Remember, If God said it—He will do it. You don't need to know how, when, or where. Just know that His word will be fulfilled.

2

No Longer an Orphan

"I will be a Father to you, and you will be my sons and daughters..."
—*2 Corinthians 6:18 (AMP)*

If we ever heard God's voice audibly, I bet most of us would freeze like a deer in headlights. Have you ever experienced it? I promise you that I would probably freeze in the moment not knowing what to do next,maybe even pee in my pants!

I've asked God numerous times to speak audibly and plainly in my frustrating seasons. Sometimes, I get tired of the parables, dreams, and visions that require interpretation. I often liken the way God speaks to me to a treasure hunt game. For those not too familiar with it, it's a fun and engaging game that consists of finding specific treasures that have been hidden in strategic spots. To find the treasures, you're given a series of clues that you need to decode. If interpreted correctly, the clues are designed to lead you to the treasures. The treasure hunt game typically requires a lot of creativity, critical thinking, and collaboration from the players.

Similar to the way my relationship with God has been over the years, very dynamic and full of interesting treasures I was tasked to find, I've come to the realization that God lives on the edge and delights in sending us on adventures while providing clues that don't always make sense to us. That's essentially my definition of living by faith.

To be fair, I see the value of the discovery process that God creates through the treasure hunt of life. He wants us to partner and collaborate with Him every step of the way by inquiring of him in our decision-making process. Simply put, God's desire has always been to do life with His children. I've been amazed by His unlimited creativity in regards to the ways He chooses to speak to us. Honestly, God blows my mind. I'm always in awe of Him and His ways. He hides hidden treasures everywhere, and yet partners with us to locate them.

Sometimes, God hides clues in friendships that will be instrumental in our current season of life. As we are obedient to develop those relationships, God uses them to mature us and releases the treasures we need for our next exploit. Spiritual clues can take on many forms, i.e. a Bible verse that speaks to you and provides guidance, a podcast host who shares an encouraging word you needed to hear at the moment, or perhaps a billboard sign that confirms what you've been sensing in your heart. God speaks in various ways and through different methods. I've learned over the years to be spiritually alert and discerning so I don't miss His clues. God's signs can literally shift the atmosphere of your heart, change your perspective, or even give you the revelation you've been seeking for years.

> *"And I will give you **treasures** hidden in the darkness — secret riches. I will do this so you may know that I am the LORD, the God of Israel, **the one who calls you by name.**" Isaiah 45:3 (NLT)*

I will never forget one of the treasures that the Lord released in my life on Friday, July 6th, 2018, but before we get to that special Friday, let me tell you what my life was like back then.

I had recently relocated to Texas (Howdy!) because the Lord had asked me to move. I had left behind everything I'd built in Maryland to start this faith journey. I was completely unsure of what life would look like in the days ahead. I had no plans, which is really not like me. I'm typically a planner and often like to have things figured out before I make any life-altering decisions.

This process was very strange to me. It was really a step of radical obedience. People move every day from one state to another, so that wasn't the biggest challenge for me. The circumstances surrounding my move were really what made me extremely nervous.

When God spoke to me and asked me to move to another state, I was without a job. I didn't have a lot of savings either. God had been preparing me for that move for a while, however, I didn't know His timing. The moment I was laid off from my previous job, I heard God's direction clearly. It was time to start packing. I thought I was getting punk'd, honestly. It felt like a really bad joke, so I thought maybe I wasn't really hearing clearly at the time. So guess what I did? I dismissed the promptings. I totally ignored the nudges of the Holy Spirit, like many of us, have done (*I know you're judging me right now*). Two months later, God's voice in my heart became even louder. I could no longer ignore it. I didn't want to be that disobedient child who refused to listen.

The truth is, I was actually terrified to take that leap of faith. I didn't want to leave everything I've ever known and start from scratch. I told God that He definitely had the wrong person. I did not have faith like Abraham. I knew that I would terribly miss my family, closest friends, and church community, but at the same time, my heart was yearning to do God's will. I was definitely in the valley of decision. I needed to make a move. I knew that I was either going to fully trust God and take the leap of faith or live in regret for the rest of my life. It took another month or so for me to muster up the courage to move. I thought I was crazy though. Who relocates 1,400 miles away from their home without any source of income and concrete plans? I decided to fully trust God, no matter what the journey ahead looked like.

My family and closest friends will tell you that I'm a very courageous person. I don't back down in the face of pain or adversity. I press on and always find the strength to move forward. Courage is perhaps one of the most important virtues we need to develop in life. Without it, I don't believe we can effectively grow the other virtues. It takes courage to love when you've been hurt. It takes courage to be vulnerable. It takes courage to stand up for what is right regardless of the pressures of life. It takes courage to forgive others even when the cut is too deep. Courage is certainly not the absence of fear but the willingness to confront it.

Friday, July 6th, 2018

It was a calm and beautiful evening. The weather was quite pleasant as I drove to my destination. A minister friend I had met not long ago on social media invited me to a prophetic church service. I didn't have anything else going on that Friday night, so I decided to go. It would be my first time to actually meet her in person. Have you ever met people and knew instantly that God was orchestrating that encounter? That's the sense I had about this particular friend. I felt in my heart that God was going to use that relationship to bless my life.

I arrived at my destination earlier than expected. It gave me an opportunity to get settled and look around before service started. The location was a quaint small church, probably with the capacity to hold 120 seats. It was an intimate atmosphere, and I could immediately sense the love of God. I sat down and watched people interact with each other before my friend arrived. I didn't quite know what to expect from the service, but I knew that I needed to hear from God. A few minutes later, my friend walked in. We hugged and were both happy to meet in person. I could tell that she would play the role of the big sister I knew I needed in that season.

The worship service started right around 7:30 pm. There was such an atmosphere of freedom in the auditorium. I could sense that the Holy Spirit was drawing me closer. It wasn't even about the songs that were being sung. There was a tangible manifestation of God's presence in that place. It was electrifying. I knew that I needed a fresh encounter with God. It felt as if God had prepared this moment just for me. I was convinced in my heart that I wasn't returning home the same way I came.

With hands lifted high and tears slowly dripping down my cheeks, I was completely lost in worship. I didn't care what I looked like to people around me. I couldn't control the outburst of pain. I began to sob uncontrollably.

All I wanted was my Father's embrace. I was undone. I was crying tears that flowed from the depth of my soul. I needed change in my life. I wasn't really sure what the change looked like. I didn't like the mental space that I was in. I knew that I needed to get out of that state of depression that was suffocating my joy. I needed a voice that was louder than the lies that were taunting me. At that moment, I knew that I needed my Heavenly Father to remind me who I was.

What happened next was the moment I didn't know I was waiting for. God spoke to me in a way I had never experienced before. I have had a lot of spiritual encounters in my Christian journey but nothing compared to what was happening. I was deeply aware that this moment of intimate worship was unique. Undoubtedly this was a kairos[3] moment - a significant defining moment in my walk with Jesus.

The Lord showed me a vision. I saw myself lying on an operating table ready to undergo an important surgical procedure. There was a surgeon fully dressed in scrubs and gloves. All I could see was his big stature but I couldn't see his face. There was a gleaming light that was radiating all around his body. He had some medical tools in his hands and he was eager to get started. As the Lord showed me that vision, I also had a knowing that I was specifically undergoing **heart surgery**. When the vision ended, I heard the Lord clearly say to me:

"You're holding on to an offense towards me, and that's why I'm giving you a new heart."

In that time of worship, it felt as if time stood still. I had no idea how long the vision lasted. I can't even remember if the worship team was still singing. All I knew was that I was in God's presence, and nothing else mattered. I can't explain the atmosphere of reverence that was created through that encounter. There aren't enough descriptive words to paint the picture so you can fully comprehend what took place in my heart that night. It was a supernatural experience. I could sense the love of God enveloping my body that night as I stood in reverence of Him. I was in awe that the Lord would bless me in that way.

That Friday night marked the beginning of my inner healing process. Somehow I knew that was the catalyst of a transformative season I was to experience. In the days and weeks following this encounter, God began to show me in detail what He was healing me from. It felt as if God was gently peeling the scales of an onion. He was progressively revealing Himself to me through the Word while peeling away the pain of my heart.

Let's take a moment and dive into the Scriptures.

> *"A new heart will I give you and a new spirit will I put within you, and I will take away the stony heart out of your flesh and **give you a heart of flesh.** And I will put my Spirit within you and cause you to walk in My statutes, and you shall heed My ordinances and do them. And you shall dwell in the land that I gave to your fathers; and you shall be My people, and I will be your God." Ezekiel 36:26-28 (AMPC)*

In this portion of the Scriptures, the Prophet Ezekiel prophesied about Israel's upcoming restoration. Up to that point, God's people have been very rebellious and idolatrous in their conduct. They were scattered through foreign lands and were dispersed among nations. When God spoke to the Israelites through Prophet Ezekiel, they were in exile during the Babylonian captivity. God, in His mercy and love for His people, promised that He would soften their hardened hearts and put His Spirit in them. This prophecy also served as a foreshadowing of the New Covenant that Jesus was to inaugurate by his death and resurrection. This was to be a sign of God's unconditional love for His people. This prophecy also highlighted God's ultimate desire for intimacy with His people. It's never been about rule-keeping and upholding a set of legal requirements. It's always been about God living in us through the power of the indwelling of His Holy Spirit. True obedience to the Father can only be birthed through deep intimacy.

Many believers who have served God for a long time sometimes find themselves in the predicament I was in. You still love the Lord but just not with the same fervency. Life happens way too often, and you've become completely numb. You find yourself going through the motions and serving God from a place of obligation. You feel as if you've done all the right things, but life hasn't compensated you fairly. At this point, you feel forgotten and utterly frustrated. Over time, you slowly begin to justify the reasons you're holding on to resentment. Your morning devotion becomes another religious exercise added to the list of the chores you need to complete for the day.

How can you resent the very person that you love so much? When life has been repeatedly unfair, you begin to filter things through the lens of your disappointments.

In that season of my life, the Lord began to expose unhealthy mindsets and lies that I had believed in. I needed to be healed from ways of thinking that were not congruent with His nature. God emphasized in that season of life that I wasn't an outcast nor abandoned. I was His and He was madly in love with me.

In Luke 15:11-32, Jesus shares a story that is widely known in the Christian community. It's the story of a certain Jewish man who had two sons. Yes, you guessed it, it's the story of the prodigal son. In this parable, the younger of the two sons asked his father for his portion of the inheritance. In ancient days, requesting an inheritance while your Father was alive would have been an insult. The giving of inheritance has always been the practice of passing on properties, estates, money, and obligations upon the death of an individual.

Requesting a heritage early would have been similar to wishing his father was dead. So, the father divided his estates and properties and gave the younger son his share. The well-funded and independent son traveled to a distant country to enjoy his newfound freedom. As he narrates the story, Jesus revealed that the younger son wasted his fortune in foolish living.

At this point, he was broke and had no means of income. He needed any job he could find to survive in a foreign land. He took a job feeding pigs. This was certainly his lowest point. How can a Jewish man feed animals that were considered to be unclean? It was at that moment that he realized that even his father's servants live well and don't go hungry. It took a pig farm for this young man to come to his senses and decide to humble himself and make the journey back to his father's house.

> *"So he got up and came to his father. But while he was still a long way off, his father saw him and was moved with compassion for him, and ran and embraced him and kissed him. And the son said to him, 'Father, I have sinned against heaven and in your sight; I am no longer worthy to be called your son.' But the father said to his servants, 'Quickly bring out the best robe [for the guest of honor] and put it on him; and give him a ring for his hand, and sandals for his feet. And bring the fattened calf and slaughter it, and let us [invite everyone and] feast and celebrate; for this son of mine was [as good as] dead and is alive again; he was lost and has been found.' So they began to celebrate" Luke 11:20-23 (AMPC).*

This portion of the Scriptures is no doubt a powerful depiction of our salvation and redemption. It reveals the love and compassion of the Father towards his children. Even when we turn our backs to God, He will always pursue us with open arms. When we repent and acknowledge our need for our Savior, God is quick to grant us the benefits that sonship provides.

But the story doesn't stop there. At this point of the story, Jesus introduces us to the older son who returned from a day's work in the field. He was completely unaware of the celebration taking place in his father's house. The music was loud, folks were dancing, and having a good time. When the older son found out that the party was in honor of his younger brother, he was livid. He refused to join the festivities and decided to stay outside. He was upset that his young brother would receive that type of honor after having squandered his inheritance in foolish living.

The father then, seeing that the older son was upset, approached him. Verses 28 through 32 reveal the rest of the story:

> *"But the elder brother became angry and deeply resentful and was not willing to go in; and his father came out and began pleading with him.* **29**

> *But he said to his father, 'Look! These many years I have served you,*
> *and I have never neglected or disobeyed your command. Yet you*
> *have never given me [so much as] a young goat, so that I might celebrate*
> *with my friends; but when this [other] son of yours arrived, who has*
> *devoured your estate with immoral women, you slaughtered the fattened*
> *calf for him!' The father said to him, 'Son, you are always with me,*
> *and all that is mine is yours. But it was fitting to celebrate and rejoice,*
> *for this brother of yours was [as good as] dead and has begun to live. He*
> *was lost and has been found." Luke 11:28-32 (AMP)*

I believe that this second half of the story is equally as important as the first half. In the passage above, Jesus essentially responds to the murmurs and complaints of the Pharisees and Scribes. Earlier in the chapter, we see in Luke 15:1-3, that these religious leaders didn't like that Jesus ate and hung out with sinners. That's why Jesus shared three different parables to teach some things and to reveal the religious and judgmental hearts that the Pharisees had.

At times in life, we behave like the oldest son and respond out of disgust and jealousy when others receive the same blessings we desire. We play God in our hearts and deem that people are unworthy of receiving God's best because of their shortcomings. Like the older son, we approach God with an entitlement mindset, pointing to the years of service we sacrificed for Him. We then begin to flaunt our obedience like a badge of honor, failing to understand that God is not looking for slaves or servants. God is looking for sons and daughters. In this parable, the older son didn't understand the proximity and access that was ALWAYS available to him. His father was always present and available. The older son wasn't an orphan nor was he an outcast. He was a son and had all the privileges that a rightful heir should have. The older son didn't know what was in his vicinity. **In his father's embrace, he was always welcomed, secure, provided for, and loved.**

Luke 15:31 is a key verse we need to highlight. The Jewish father said to his oldest son, *"Son, you are always with me, and all that is mine is yours."* It reminds me of the message Jesus shared with his disciples when he was

29

preparing them to welcome the promised Holy Spirit upon his departure from the earth.

> *"But when He, the Spirit of Truth (the Truth-giving Spirit) comes, He will guide you into all the Truth (the whole, full Truth). For He will not speak His own message [on His own authority]; but He will tell whatever He hears [from the Father; He will give the message that has been given to Him], and He will announce and declare to you the things that are to come [that will happen in the future].*
>
> *He will honor and glorify Me, because He will take of (receive, draw upon) what is Mine and will reveal (declare, disclose, transmit) it to you.*
>
> ***Everything that the Father has is Mine. That is what I meant when I said that He [the Spirit] will take the things that are Mine and will reveal (declare, disclose, transmit) it to you." John 16:13-15***

In this passage, Jesus emphasizes that everything the Father has also belongs to Him. He reveals the oneness that exists between Him and the Father, and Jesus invites us to partake of His relationship with the Father through the Holy Spirit. Jesus is essentially saying that we also can be totally unified with the Father through His Holy Spirit. Everything the Father has is also ours because we're co-heirs with Christ. (Romans 8:17)

In the parable we read, the oldest son needed a revelation of true sonship. He needed to understand that He didn't have to slave his way into being loved by his daddy. He needed to understand that he was celebrated and loved simply because he was a son. Many believers who come from religious backgrounds have a faulty idea that God is an authoritative and controlling master.

Because of the unhealthy religious standards they uphold, they often feel as if they never measure up. A lot of Christians, who seem to think that way also have a performance-based mindset, often measure how good their relationship with God is by the religious activities they perform for the church. As a result, when they fall short of that standard, they often deal with feelings of guilt, inadequacy, and rejection.

In his book, Relational Intelligence, Dr. Dharius Daniels discusses what he calls rejection infection. He says, *"When rejection is not properly dealt with, it can produce a wound to our soul that affects our sense of self. A soul wound is dangerous because the bleeding is internal and invisible. These kinds of wounds are often underestimated and overlooked. When we don't take soul wounds seriously, we end up putting band-aids in places that actually need stitches."*[4]

We've all experienced rejection at one point in our lives. Whether it was a relationship that turned sour or a promotion that we didn't get, rejection can be very painful. It doesn't matter who you are; we've all felt the sting of it. I'd like to point out that there's a difference between having gone through rejection once or twice in your life and being oppressed by the spirit of rejection. Those are two different things. We understand that there's a demonic world working against the children of God with the mission to oppress and destroy our lives.

The Scripture tells us that Satan's mission is to steal, kill, and destroy; however, Jesus came to give us abundant life (John 10:10). That's why we have to be discerning and aware of the enemy's tactics at all times. One of the ways the enemy robs us of our joy and peace is by releasing the spirit of rejection.

The spirit of rejection takes advantage of the unprocessed trauma in our lives for the purpose of digging a deeper wound. It attaches itself to a negative experience we've had and magnifies its effect. If you come from a broken marriage or have experienced any type of neglect in life, that spirit will look for opportunities to oppress you so you never mature to your full potential in Christ.

The Bible is clear that we're not wrestling against flesh and blood but against demonic powers and forces who are using strategies of deception, distraction, and manipulation. But thank God, we have spiritual weapons at our disposal to stand against the enemy and his cohorts. We need to remember that the enemy excels at lying. After all, the Bible calls him the father of lies. That's why the spirit of rejection is a lie from the pit of hell.

When the spirit of rejection tells you that you're unwanted, that you don't deserve to be loved, or that no one is interested in what you bring to the

31

table, you've got to stand up against it and fight. Fight against every feeling of worthlessness and dejection. Fight with the Sword of the Spirit, which is the truth of God's Word. Fight from a place of victory. Christ has already won the battle; you just need to reinforce it by standing on God's word.

Healing for Our Souls

The soul is a three-part living organism composed of the mind, the will, and the emotions. From our upbringing into adulthood, we develop worldviews and patterns of thinking that shape our behaviors and life's decisions. Those mindsets we've picked up over time dictate our human interactions and influence our spiritual experiences. Our culture is intentional in feeding us ideologies that support their agendas - from what is taught in school to the type of promotional ads we ingest. These mentalities often stunt our growth and are contrary to our identity in Christ.

Orphan Mindset

Orphan mindset is used here figuratively as a mindset or belief system based on rejection, separation, abandonment, or even lack of trust. This way of thinking produces behaviors that mirror that of an orphan. Oftentimes, people who exhibit those characteristics don't always feel that they can depend on anyone; they often feel abandoned and have a tendency to always be in survival mode. They have this idea that they constantly need to look out for themselves because of their inability to trust others with their lives. The term - orphan mindset - is not used in any derogatory context in regards to those who are orphaned in real life. The orphan mindset denotes a fatherlessness state and patterns of thinking that mirror that of an orphan. We've all felt abandoned at some point in life, been rejected, or experienced the illusion of separation from God.

The enemy wants us to believe that we still need to earn our way into salvation. That's one of his deceptive plots. Many believers have a difficult time embracing the gift of Sonship and Daughtership because they often feel undeserving of God's perfect love. At times, we still operate under a rule-keeping system and a religious mindset that brings condemnation and not freedom in Christ. God wants us to break free from the old covenant mindset and receive new life through Christ. The Scriptures tell us that Jesus came to fulfill the law (Matthew 5:17). In other words, without Jesus' sacrifice, death, and resurrection, no one could live a moral life.

The Covenant of Grace, or the New Covenant that was established through Jesus' death and resurrection, reconciled and restored us back to God's original plan. Intimacy with God has always been the original intention. I don't know about you, but I'm really thankful for God's redemptive nature. Galatians 4 states it so beautifully:

> *"But when [in God's plan] the proper time had fully come, God sent His Son, born of a woman, born under the [regulations of the] Law, so that He might redeem and liberate those who were under the Law, that we [who believe] might be adopted as sons [as God's children with all rights as fully grown members of a family]." Galatians 4:4-5*

We are not spiritual orphans nor slaves to a religious system; we're adopted sons and daughters of God. Jesus came to fulfill the requirements of the law, so we no longer have to live in shame, sin, fear, or condemnation. In Christ, we're free indeed. People who have an orphan mindset are motivated by performance, in order to gain love and acceptance. Living from a place of performance only magnifies our insecurities. Because spiritual orphans are plagued with this sense of unworthiness, they don't believe that they can hear the voice of God. A spiritual orphan is often under the oppression of the spirit of condemnation and guilt.

Characteristics Of An Orphan Mindset:

- Often deals with insecurities and fear

- Lives a lonely and isolated life
- Often deals with self-esteem issues
- Draws his/her identity from external sources such as their work, achievements, or people's praises
- Has the tendency to be excessively independent or extremely dependent on others
- Self-protecting and will do anything to preserve themselves
- Has difficulty being fruitful in relationships because he/she has a hard time trusting others

To be clear, there is no such thing as an orphan **"spirit"** in the scriptures. The term used here is orphan **"mindset"**, indicating that this specific belief system can be changed (in contrast with a spirit that often needs to be cast out). The scriptures talk about the importance of renewing our minds in the Word of God and having the ability to think like Christ. On earth, Jesus Christ was close to His Heavenly Father. It's evident that He was one with the Father. Christ was thinking like His father. If indeed we're hidden in Christ, we also have the ability to think like Christ. Thus, anything that is not in alignment with Christ's mindset is not from God.

That's why the enemy, who is the master illusionist, excels in sowing seeds of doubts and lies in our mind that create an illusion of separation. The Scriptures tell us that the enemy doesn't have the ability to tell the truth. His character contains no truth. He's studied humankind since creation and has perfected his deceptive schemes.

In her Bible Study "The Armor of God", Author Priscilla Shirer gives a powerful description of our adversary. She says, *"The enemy's overarching device is deception. He shades reality with enticing and alluring colors, seducing us away from black-and-white principles. He propagates fantasies causing temporal and insignificant things to somehow appear immensely valuable and favorable. He hides consequences in the fine print while highlighting only the parts that appeal to our short-sighted self-gratifying flesh. His packaging is so clever that unless we know what's true - I mean really know it, know it at our core we easily fall prey to his ploys."*[5]

As children of God, it's imperative that the truth of the Word of God takes root in our hearts to enable us to stand against the plots of the evil one. Many of us succumbed to his lies and have accepted those as our mode of operating. We need to uproot and dismantle those lies one by one with the truth of the Word of God. It's time to take the Sword of the Spirit, which is the word of God, and dig out those lies. You're not rejected. You're not separated from God. In Christ, you're more than enough. You're forgiven. Your sins, and mine, are tossed into the sea of forgetfulness when we repent. The master illusionist can no longer condemn nor accuse you when you fully walk in the Spirit of Sonship. You're not a slave, nor an orphan; you are a son or daughter of the living God.

Slave Mentality

Because we live in a world that doesn't uphold God's ways of thinking, we can at times be under its influence. There are other mindsets or thinking patterns that cause us to become slaves to cultural norms and people's opinions. Our western ideologies often promote individualism and an independent mindset that often interferes with our relationship with God. We have this idea that we know what's best for us and that somehow we think we don't need God's help. Sometimes, as believers, we walk around thinking we can figure things out, and we neglect to involve God's wisdom in our daily decisions. We fail to understand that a self-reliant posture hinders intimacy and interdependence with God. That's why Scriptures encourage us to renew our minds in the Word of God and not to adopt unhealthy patterns of thinking that are prevalent in our world today. (Romans 12:2)

The world believes in striving for praise, approval, and acceptance of man. No wonder why we're so obsessed with celebrities and sometimes put people on pedestals. Sometimes we live for people's applause to the point that it motivates our actions. The truth is, many are waiting for people to approve and validate their purpose before they take action. Let's be real and say it like it is. If you're waiting for people to applaud you, you'll likely go to the grave with your talents and untapped potential. We were created to worship God; however, the idols of this world have taken God's place in the hearts of men. That's why it's no surprise that even in the church, believers are promoting their own agendas and glorifying their own kingdoms.

Also, when we operate in a slave mentality, we have a tendency to want to control the process. We begin to wrestle with whether God truly knows what's best for us. Believers who have a difficult time letting go of control, are often eager to also control the outcome of the situation they find themselves in. Our desire to control the outcome reveals that we don't truly trust God. Sons completely abandon their will to the Lordship of Christ. We need to grow in our capacity to trust God with all the details of our lives. Trusting that in God's infinite wisdom, He knows the outcome that will best serve His purposes and advance His Kingdom. In other words, God has our back, and He can always be trusted.

People-Pleasing Mentality

Another unfruitful mindset we begin to adopt when we don't know who we are as sons and daughters is a people-pleasing mentality. When we're motivated to please people, it often leads to a life of anxiety, frustration, and fear. In fact, the Word declares in Proverbs:

> *"The fear of man brings a snare, but whoever leans on, trusts in, and puts his confidence in the Lord is safe and set on high." Proverbs 29:25*

Let's look at the definition of the word "snare." According to the Merriam-Webster dictionary, a snare is a noose, a trap, or cord often used to entangle birds or mammals. When we look at the scriptures again, we can deduce that the fear of man leads to captivity and bondage. Perhaps the greatest prison that people live in today is the fear of people's opinions and perceptions. The Bible tells us that the presence of fear is an indication that God's love hasn't fully matured in our hearts. 1 John 4:18 tells us that perfect love casts out all fear. The fear that is mentioned in this context deals with the spirit of fear, not to be confused with the fear of the Lord, which will be discussed later in "Identity of True Sonship."

Common Traits Of a People-Pleasing Mentality:

- Afraid of being rejected or abandoned
- Preoccupied about what others think and feel
- Fearful of saying no
- Seeking people's approval
- Overwork themselves and have a poor work-life balance
- Often struggle with being authentic
- Often commit to things out of obligation
- Often has a difficult time putting themselves first

Performance-Obsessed Mentality

Another widespread mentality that is prevalent in our culture today is the idea of a high-performance culture. A culture is essentially belief systems, core values, and ideologies that influence the behaviors and lifestyles of a specific group of people. In our society today, we've created businesses and companies that focus on making sure people are highly effective in their roles. Systems have been put in place to measure progress, monitor teams, and personal goals. A performance culture is heavily based on discipline, accountability, and a high pursuit of excellence. Often, in performance-driven organizations, good behaviors are incentivized and reinforced, while any ideas or behaviors that challenge the status quo are obstructed. In some organizations, who adopt a performance-focused approach, there could be a tendency to exert excessive control and demand results at any cost.

Just like in anything in life, there are pros and cons associated with any concept. Generally speaking, a high-performance culture fosters increased productivity in the workforce, which ultimately leads to higher profits. While a performance-based culture can help businesses and corporations achieve their desired results, it can also create unhealthy environments when misused. In the absence of balance, high-performance cultures can create environments that stifle employees' growth while focusing only on the bottom line. A highly competitive environment can lead individuals to prove themselves by any means necessary and become obsessed over numbers and achievements. When the focus is on achieving success at any cost, companies and organizations end up creating fear-based environments. Individuals can become afraid of failure to the point that they will put their integrity on the line and make poor decisions.

To create a more balanced culture in the workplace, leadership teams of successful companies are now proactively encouraging a growth mindset. Individuals and teams who adopt this way of thinking aim at investing in their employees by encouraging learning, character development, and maximizing potential. When companies promote growth, hard work, motivation, and continuous improvement, they have a better chance to create healthy thriving environments.

In my younger days, I had the opportunity to work in the nonprofit sector for a large ministry on the East Coast. During my tenure there, I observed the negative impacts that a high-performance mindset produced in the lives of people who loved God. Individuals who initially started their journey with the desire to serve God's people became obsessed with numbers, applause, and recognition. Their desire for results fostered a sense of unhealthy competition within the organization. Some became so obsessed with the idea of success, their personal agendas, and being perceived as successful that they engaged in unethical behaviors. When the motivation behind our pursuit is not wholesome, it can have a negative impact on our character and even our relationships.

In the Bible days, Jesus' disciples were also ordinary men, just like us. They all had personal strengths and weaknesses. These were men who accomplished great exploits but also made poor decisions. During a regular day in ministry, the disciples were arguing about who was the greatest in the

Kingdom. They were going back and forth amongst themselves to determine the criteria of greatness. I would imagine perhaps they were discussing who amongst them was better known in Galilee or Capernaum.

In our modern-day, I'm sure they would be fussing about who was the most influential on Instagram, who received the biggest honorarium during the course of the year, or who had the most campus locations. Jesus always amazes me in the ways he led and taught his disciples.

In Mark 9:35, Jesus sat down with the disciples for a mentoring session. He proceeded to tell them that whoever wants to be first must take the last place and become a servant leader. Then Jesus asked a child to come in their midst so he could emphasize his lesson. In that moment, Jesus demonstrated what greatness looks like. Greatness is revealed through the innocence, meekness, and humility of a child. (Mark 9:35-36)

I believe we need to beware of cultures and mindsets that promote an un-healthy, non-balanced lifestyle. We shouldn't allow societal culture to define for us what success and greatness should look like in our lives. Nowadays, folks glamorize being busy and overworking themselves. Somehow we feel important when our schedules are booked and boast about our non-existent sleep habits. It's no doubt that many of these societal mindsets crept into the church and in many ways hinder our relationship with our Heavenly Father. God is not looking for individuals who will slave themselves to feel significant or loved.

Too many people serve to promote their own agendas and pursuits. Believers who operate with a performance-based mindset often strive their way into God's love. Their need for significance is often drawn from how much work or service they perform for God. Performers have a tendency to base their identity on what they do and how well they do it. They are often highly judgmental individuals who are extremely hard on themselves and sometimes difficult to work with because of their perfectionist tendencies. Spiritual sons and daughters of God are secure in God and are valued not just because of what they do but because of who they are.

Understand that it's commendable to be a person who values productivity, drive, and who thrives at getting things done. I'm all for a lifestyle that produces focus, determination, excellence, and great habits. However, we have to ensure that we don't develop unhealthy mindsets which can lead us to a life of bondage. What our culture desperately needs today are sons and daughters of God with pure hearts who understand the mandate of being about the Father's business.

Our relationship with the Lord should never be based on performance; it's founded on intimate friendship. Religion keeps a record of rights and wrongs; whereas, an authentic relationship with God is based on sonship through the love of the Father. Many of us haven't fully experienced the love of the Father - that's why we condemn ourselves in so many areas of our lives. God wants us to experience His forgiveness and grace as we grow deeper in His love.

Through my healing journey, the Lord wasn't just interested in dismantling the unfruitful mindsets I was operating in. His aim was also to expose and uproot the bitterness that was causing my heart to grow cold. The head surgeon was on a mission to remove my diseased heart and replace it with His.

The Danger of Bitterness

In the previous chapter, we addressed unprocessed disappointment and how to heal from it. A disappointment left untreated can further create an offense. An offense that has fully taken roots in our hearts becomes bitterness. Holding on to hurt and bitterness is not the response of a son or daughter of God. The scriptures encourage us to imitate Jesus and mirror his character and heart posture. Jesus taught us to love and to forgive others, as our Heavenly Father has forgiven us.

When we allow bitterness to fester in our hearts, we begin to slowly become lukewarm towards God. Our sensitivity to the nudges of the Holy Spirit diminishes as we begin to pull further away from God. It's a dangerous place to be. Bitterness produces spiritual death and even medically speaking, bitterness is at the root of ulcers and other medical conditions. When you find yourself becoming lukewarm and gradually becoming indifferent to the voice of God, it's a clear indication that your relationship with God is not where it needs to be.

There are some telltale signs that reveal that we might be developing a stony heart towards God:

- When we begin to entertain temptations by putting ourselves in compromising situations
- When we are no longer sensitive to God's promptings
- When we no longer respond to the conviction of the Holy Spirit
- When we begin to justify our sins and minimize the impact of any choice that displeases God
- When we aren't excited about participating in church activities or gathering with other believers
- When we become negative and cynical in our interactions with people
- When we no longer have the joy of the Lord nor the excitement of testifying of God's goodness
- When our past lifestyle and choices start seducing us
- When we deliberately re-visit relationships that God told us to discard and stay away from
- When we begin to justify the reason why we shouldn't forgive others

This list is by no means an exhaustive one; these are just some of the symptoms that take place when we allow bitterness to take root in the soil of our hearts. We become numb and desensitized to the presence of God. God doesn't want us to give room to bitterness. There's a reason why God tells us to watch over our heart because out of it flows the issues of life. What we plant in the soil of our hearts is what will ultimately grow and affect every area of our lives. So, we have to be mindful of the kind of seeds that we choose to plant. A seed will produce after its kind, so an offended heart cannot speak words of life.

Healing Doesn't Happen Overnight

In this painful season that I was in, I needed to fully understand that God would never set me up to fail. I needed to allow God to cut the root of the bitterness that was in my heart. I needed to trust God with my pain. Being the good Father that God is, He takes care of us as we journey through every season.

You know, I grew up in church. Early on as a believer, I've learned that God said in His word that He will never leave me nor forsake me, but did I really believe that God actually meant it? That's the real question. There were moments in my healing process when I couldn't sense God's presence at all. I wasn't in sin nor was I away from Him, but God was unusually quiet.

I remember days when I would even question the status of my relationship with God. I mean, after walking with God for 15 years, I couldn't understand the type of season that I was in. It was a painful season for sure. There would be days when I could ball my eyes out. I felt that God was giving me the silent treatment on purpose, not knowing what I did to merit that type of behavior. It was confusing to me as if my Heavenly Father turned His back at me. I began to question the love of the Father and His ability to not only care for me but provide for me. I was in an awful place despite the encounter I had on that fateful Friday night. My healing journey didn't happen overnight. It wasn't instantaneous. It was a journey.

Listen, I always say that the Christian journey is no walk in the park. It gets real. We have real emotions. We go through painful circumstances that will test every single tenet of our faith. In my case, I was entertaining the lies that Satan was throwing at me. I was under attack, and I knew it but didn't understand why God wasn't delivering me from those attacks when I was doing all the "right" spiritual disciplines. We pray, we fast, we seek to live a holy life, and we live our good quiet Christian lives and expect God to hold His end of the bargain—isn't it how we often think sometimes?

Every single one of us will go through seasons in which our faith will be tested. In most cases, the test will be to authenticate our faith. In my case, it felt as if I was in a season within a season. I was in a healing process while my faith in God was being tested.

We have a very limited understanding of God's will for our lives, and we often don't understand God's ways or methods. God doesn't operate based on our human intellect; He is far superior to our intelligence or human wisdom. The methods that God uses to unfold His plans in our lives at times will not make sense to our natural intelligence because God sees the end from the beginning. He sees situations and scenarios from all angles, as he is orchestrating the details of our lives and is aligning them to His perfect will.

The problem is that we subconsciously think that we are better equipped to figure out the occurrences of our life. We are not even able to predict our tomorrow, no one knows what joys or challenges the next day will bring, so why do we sometimes think that we can figure out our lives? God took me out of my hometown into a new city so he could heal my wounded soul. The truth is, growth only happens outside of our comfort zone - so does our wholeness. If this was the only reason for my move, it would still be worth it.

Just like Abraham, God told me to go into a "foreign" land, so he could establish His covenant with me. This was to be a love encounter I had never experienced before. It was time to embrace a new dimension of the gift of sonship. As God instructed Abraham to circumcise his male descendants on the eighth day as a sign of the covenant with him, the Lord also circumcised my heart.

> *"And the Lord your God will circumcise your hearts and the hearts of*
> *your descendants, to love the Lord your God with all your [mind and]*
> *heart and with all your being, that you may live." Deuteronomy 30:6*

My "heart surgery" was a painful, but necessary process I had to experience. It allowed me to grow in trusting the Father's heart on a deeper level.

Prophetic Declaration

Strengthen Your Core

I almost gave up.

I almost quit fighting.

I almost stopped believing because of the weight of the warfare in my life.

Listen - you see people's glory, but you don't know the reality of the turmoil behind the scenes. When the curtains are closed, you have no idea of the fight backstage.

You don't know the private battles people face in order to stand tall in public. Quit judging and ask God to help you develop greater compassion to love people like Christ does.

This is my story. Christ is strengthening my core. I've gone through some trauma and trials that almost took me out of the race. Literally.

But God, His strength, and the reality of His calling upon my life would not let me quit. We're more than conquerors in Christ alone.

Strengthen your core and stand in the truth. Anchor your soul in the unfailing word of God, because there's a day coming when your root system will be tested. Trust me.

Life has a way of shaking your entire belief system.

Make sure you're firmly rooted in Christ daily.

I smile today because the battles can't kill me. I stand in the might of the Almighty One.

Fight until you have the victory! Don't quit. Generations are depending on your ability to TRIUMPH.

> *"And after you have suffered a little while, the God of all grace, who has called you to his eternal glory in Christ, will himself restore, confirm, strengthen, and establish you." 1 Peter 5:10*

3

The Bride Price

"You're loved by a God who engraved your name on the palms of His hands."
—*Dumbi Mabiala*

I grew up a devout Catholic; regularly attending catechism classes and mass was part of my weekly activities. My mother religiously took us to church on Sundays and prioritized all Catholic sacraments from baptism to confirmation. Prayer was also a big deal in our home. I remember mom would gather us so we could worship and read the Psalms together and go through the rosary. I can't tell you the numbers of Hail Mary's and Our Father's I recited over the years.

My siblings and I were fully immersed in the faith early on in our upbringing, but we didn't fully comprehend any of those religious practices. It's interesting how one could be so close to the truth and yet have no revelation of it. How many scholars of our days have exegesis biblical texts and studied historical facts but still are so far away from God. You can grow up memorizing and quoting the entire Bible without ever experiencing the intimacy and the tangible power of the Holy Spirit. For many of us, our backgrounds were rooted in religious traditions and practices that promoted a form of godliness without God's power. You've heard the saying, *"just because you go to church, it doesn't make you a Christian."* I've found that statement to be so true.

What a sad reality to know that the god of this age has blinded the minds and spiritual sights of so many, so that they cannot discern the truth of who Christ is. 2 Corinthians 4:3 says the truth is veiled to those who are perishing. As believers, it's our mandate to consistently pray for those whose eyes have been blinded by Satan.

Jesus spoke to the multitude in John 8:32 and declared:

> *"And you shall **know the truth**, and **the truth shall make you free."***

In this statement, Jesus was emphasizing that there's tremendous liberty available to each of us when we are knowledgeable of who He is as **The Truth**. Freedom from sins, bondage, and shame is only possible when the truth is in operation in our lives.

When we study the root of the word "know" that Jesus used in this statement, we find out that its transliteration is *"ginōskō"*, which is a Greek word for perceive, to become acquainted with, to have knowledge of. I also find it interesting that when you further study this word *"ginōskō"*, it is also a Jewish idiom for sexual intercourse between a man and a woman (Strong's G1097, Blue Letter Bible). Perhaps Jesus was intentional in the way that He used this word to indicate that we ought to intimately become one with the truth.

Back in the days, I admired my mother's spiritual discipline (and I still do to this day). Although, I don't believe that she had a personal relationship with the Lord Jesus at the time. Looking back, it was apparent that God was drawing her closer to Himself. Mom was aware that it was very important to expose her children to the discipline that religion provides. I believe that Mom absolutely instilled a reverence for God early on in my life. To this day, I'm so grateful that my mother made sure we had a spiritual foundation.

Although I knew of God, I didn't know God intimately. There is a big difference between the two, as we discussed earlier in this chapter. At the time, I didn't have a personal relationship with Jesus as I do now. I had a tremendous reverence and respect towards God, but it didn't come from a place of intimate worship. It was based on fear.

Back then, I knew that whatever I did in life, I wanted to make sure that I was on good terms with the Man upstairs. I remember as a child, I hated being in trouble, so early on I started developing perfectionist tendencies. I wanted to conduct myself in a perfect way from a moral standpoint. I always wanted to be above reproach. I remember being aware that I didn't want God nor my parents to ever be upset with me. How unrealistic was that?!

I was just one of those kids who was fearful of getting in trouble. I was scared of the consequences, so that definitely motivated my "good" behavior. I was definitely not a mischievous child. I was the studious and reserved kind. I wanted to always do everything by the book so that everyone would always be pleased with me. So I was determined to do what it took to stay on good terms with God and my parents.

As a kid, I often felt like an outcast. I never really felt that I fit in. It's interesting; looking back, I now understand the reason why I was never really part of any cliques in school. I would hang out with different kids, but I didn't have an inner circle that I was a part of. I grew up extremely shy and timid, fearful of people's perceptions of me. I felt as if I didn't have a voice. I was totally scared to speak up in class, even when I knew the answers. I didn't value what I had to say nor did I know the power of my voice at such a young age. I couldn't stand up for myself. I remember wishing that I had an older brother who could defend, protect, and look after me, but I was the oldest child amongst my siblings. Early on, I felt the pressure and the responsibility of setting the standard in academics and moral values. Somehow, the pressure to set the standard was already ingrained in me from a very young age.

Growing up, I always wanted to be a daddy's girl. I had tremendous respect and admiration for my dad and the line of work he was involved in. I wanted to be well-rounded, highly educated, and well-traveled just like my dad. Yes, my dad traveled a whole bunch. Over the decades, he filled several passports and would always bring me back currencies from various nations. That's when I started collecting money from different parts of the world. I believe that's when God began to birth in me a desire to study different cultures.

My dad would be gone for long periods of time. He certainly worked hard at providing for us and made sure we were financially stable as a family. I'm really grateful for the investment and sacrifices he made for our family. However, I remember being jealous of my friends back then who appeared to have had a close relationship with their fathers. I would have given anything for that type of relationship with my father. I remember I wanted a real friendship with him. I wanted to be able to discuss some of the emotional things I was going through as a child or even silly things that teenagers like to talk about.

That's not the type of relationship we had at the time. My dad has always been an intellectual person and a great communicator. He's been good at giving my siblings and I great wisdom on future career paths we were interested in or his take on current events and political matters. He would often share with us some of his findings and research in regards to his work. No doubt that our conversations were highly educational and enlightening.

On several occasions, he would discuss the research regarding HIV and AIDS, since he was working in the public health space at the time. He would talk to us about sex education, prevention, and condom campaigns he was involved in. Hmm. Those discussions were really uncomfortable to sit through at times. It was a little bit awkward to hear my father talk about condoms and other contraceptive methods. However, those lectures provided us with the information we needed to make good decisions as we got older. In my case, after hearing about AIDS that many times, I made up my mind to stay abstinent. It felt easier at the time to choose that route.

Every family has its issues and mine was no different. The challenges we were navigating as a family made it difficult to connect with my dad on an emotional level. However, over the years, I've witnessed the hand of God weaving hearts together and slowly bringing healing, forgiveness, and restoration into my family. It's been a work in progress, and I celebrate the healing that's taking place in my family. As an adult, I thank God for the relationship I'm still developing with my father.

My mother was the one holding down the fort while my dad was away.

She was present and very involved in raising us. She wore many different hats and did it with so much poise, love, and determination.

Early on, my mom sacrificed a lot, putting her dreams on hold and devoting her time to invest in us. She always ensured my siblings and I were completely cared for. I think we don't give enough credit to the selfless work that stay-at-home mothers or working mothers do for their families. It's a shame that sometimes we take our mothers for granted. I've been blessed with a mother who is my greatest cheerleader, a spiritual advisor, our home manager, our purpose pusher, and also a great disciplinarian. Oh yes, you don't play with my mother! She raised us in a strict manner and was always a no-nonsense person. Her tough love provided the structure and discipline that helped us become mature and responsible adults. I've experienced Mom's tough love on numerous occasions, even though I was trying so hard to stay out of trouble.

There's one particular incident I'll never forget. I was probably fifteen years old. I had secretly started dating this guy in our neighborhood (sorry mom, I never told you!). It was a Saturday afternoon, and mom had asked me to start boiling some kidney beans while she was at the store. I remember filling the cooking pot with enough water and putting the beans on the stove to a low simmer, so they could cook slowly. Then I got a phone call from my boyfriend, who wanted to see me for a few minutes.

Well, I figured there was enough water in the pot and that I wasn't going to be out for too long, so I went to meet my boyfriend and spent some time with him. Minutes turned into a whole hour, and I had completely forgotten about those beans. When my brain finally remembered I had left some beans on the stove, my heart started pounding so hard. I started sprinting back to the house, probably as fast as Usain Bolt. I had to run as fast as a gazelle to get to the house before my mom did. When I made it to the house, to my surprise, my mom was already there. My heart almost skipped a beat. I didn't know what to do. I started crying and shaking in fear. I couldn't believe I almost burned down the house. My mom had arrived just in time to turn off the stove. Isn't God good? It could have been a different story, but thank God, she arrived just in time.

But let me tell you the type of whooping I received that day... My buttocks will never forget the pain they experienced. Yes, my mom believes in belts and using wooden spatulas to spank our behinds. I know that spanking is a big debate in parenting these days and some of you may not be comfortable with the idea, but just know that I turned out to be ok. I can definitely tell you that I learned my lesson that day. For sure.

I had extremely low self-esteem in my teen years. I was full of insecurities, and I had no sense of identity at the time. The voice in my head would always echo negative and condemning thoughts. I couldn't dare look at anybody in their eyes, because I didn't have the courage to confront their opinions of me. See, I was also bullied on numerous occasions and for various reasons. From having a unique name to being a young girl who experienced puberty at such an early age. As a kid, I was chubby and curvy. I had a poor self-image and didn't like my body type. I thought I had way too many curves. I was also heavily chested early in my teens. I experienced all of those hormonal changes much earlier than most of my friends who entered puberty later in their adolescent years. At nine years old, I already had a menstrual cycle. Crazy, isn't it? So physically, it was quite apparent that I was developing faster than my classmates. Naturally, I became the target of the bullies who were mocking me incessantly.

Back when I was growing up, there was a popular cartoon that kids were watching at the time, called "Dumbo the flying elephant." If you're not familiar with this cartoon, it's a 1941 American animated film produced by Walt Disney. It's an old-action cartoon that has been re-adapted over the years. In the film, the main character is Jumbo Jr., who's a young circus elephant born with comically large ears. In the movie, he's taunted by a group of kids who cruelly nickname him "Dumbo," as in "dumb." Although Jumbo Jr. is ridiculed for his big ears, he later finds out that he's capable of flying by using his ears as wings. Back then, in school, kids would ask me why my parents picked such a name for me. Every time teachers would call on me and say my name out loud, kids would chuckle and refer to me as Dumbo, the flying elephant. It was quite humiliating and especially painful when teachers weren't correcting the bullies. I've had several of those embarrassing moments over the course of my childhood.

As I grew older, I thought those mockeries would cease. I was completely wrong about that. It persisted even in adulthood. I've had colleagues in the workplace poke fun at my name and mispronounce it on purpose. I've learned over the years that people sometimes choose to be ignorant. The best way to deal with such people is to choose the higher road. I wasn't going to stoop low and entertain their stupidity. Because of the bullying I've experienced over those years, it took me some time to find the courage to stand up for myself and finally be proud of my name.

Now, I can't tell you how much I love the uniqueness and beauty of my name. Especially that I was named after my paternal grandmother, which makes the name even more significant. It's a very authentic name and quite exotic. Dumbi, which is pronounced "doom-bee", means to **bring to life** or **to give birth to.** What a powerful meaning! I always like to say that I was born to give birth to God's amazing promises. I've seen God use me in many ways to speak life over people and to produce fruits that glorify Him.

You can probably tell that I wasn't part of the popular crew as a kid. My nerdy, tom-boyish look on a curvy body didn't help at all. The Steve Urkel glasses that I was wearing at the time didn't exactly make me attractive. I know most people who know me personally today can't believe that I had a tom-boyish phase of life. I sure did. I didn't really like to wear dresses, and I didn't think I looked exceptionally feminine at the time. So I had no chance—especially not competing with the pretty girls in school, who effortlessly had the attention of the guys who never really glanced at me. I can't believe that I had this level of poor self-esteem. I didn't know who I was. I didn't know my worth or my value back then. I can't believe I spent my entire elementary and middle school years in obscurity because I was way too timid to speak up. If I can be totally honest, I really didn't think I mattered to anyone.

I knew my family cared about me, but that didn't really count since the family that we're born into is forced to accept us. Your family didn't get to pick you. After all, God determines the type of family each of us is born into, right? It's so embarrassing to admit all the insecurities that were enveloping my skin. It felt like a plague. I really didn't like myself very much. I wanted to be beautiful, extremely intelligent, and desired.

Back then, I'm sure I didn't have the appropriate language to correctly express what I was feeling internally. All I remember is that I wasn't a very happy child. I wanted to be seen, loved, and accepted. Sometimes when I sit and think about all the lies of the enemies I had believed about myself, I rise up in deep anger. Satan always seeks to convince us that we're worthless, dejected, unimportant, or a victim of our circumstances.

The Word of God, on the other hand, always points us to God's heart concerning us. The truth is, we are more than conquerors in Christ. We are not abandoned or rejected. We are accepted in the Father's embrace. We're God's treasured possession and the apple of His eyes.

As the oldest of three children, early on I felt the burden of being the little mama of the house. Again, you don't necessarily choose your birth order in your family. Around the age of nine, I was nicknamed *"Mami"* which means little mama, and can I tell you that I absolutely hated the name? I didn't want to be a little mama; I wanted to be a kid with no responsibility.

In the African culture, it's expected for the parents to train the oldest girl child to care for, watch over her younger siblings, and learn her way around the kitchen along with other domestic work. I do believe that my parents did an exceptional job of instilling in me, early on, a sense of responsibility in regards to my siblings. There was no doubt in my mind that I was my brother's and sister's keeper. I think I took that job way too seriously though. So at times, I was the mean older sister who was strict, rigid, and demanded perfection from her younger ones.

As far as perfectionism is concerned, I might have inherited that mindset from my mom. She can attest to the fact that it was quite a task to please her growing up. If the bed wasn't perfectly tucked in, it wasn't good enough. If the game room wasn't spotless and toys well organized in a corner of the room, it wasn't good enough. It seemed as if things were never perfect enough for Mom.

There was always room for improvement whether it was our grades or our cooking skills. Dad also was very strict with us in terms of our school, grades, and reading habits. He would always remind us that we had the privilege to go to all these private schools and that it didn't come cheap. We had to bring home good grades.

What I'm most grateful for in regards to my upbringing, was my exposure to different countries. My dad has worked for several international organizations over the years, which provided my family and I tremendous opportunities to live in various nations. My siblings and I still have such a deep appreciation for cultures, diversity, and languages. In fact, we grew up speaking several languages around the house. From French to Lingala, English, or Spanish—which we picked up while we were living in the Dominican Republic - a normal day in our house felt like walking through an international market. And as I got older, it was no surprise to me the type of friendships I attracted into my life. Some of my best friends are from Japan, India, Nigeria, the UK, and Kenya. It's truly enriching to surround yourself with people from different cultural backgrounds and worldviews.

While we lived in West Africa, at the tender age of 12, I was introduced to pornography. I vividly remember the day my innocence was stolen from me. My parents were not home. Dad was out of the country, and Mom was running errands. Our nanny was watching us that day. She walked into our living room and showed me a sexual magazine, then she popped a pornographic video in the VHS player. At first, I was shocked by the imagery that I was looking at. Then I became intrigued as these images started producing feelings I had never felt before.

From that moment on, the spirit of lust awakened sexual desires that were never designed to be awakened at such an early age. From that point on until about my mid-twenties, I secretly became addicted to porn. For years, I was indulging in that sin. I was ashamed of what I was doing; I knew it was wrong. Despite the fact that I didn't have a personal relationship with Jesus while I was engaged in that behavior, my conscience knew right from wrong. It was unholy and completely wrong. I didn't know how to stop it, and frankly, at the time, I didn't want to stop watching it because of how it made me feel.

Statistics show that there is a growing number of people addicted to porn nowadays. With the accessibility and affordability of the internet over the past few decades, porn sites have seen a rising number of visitors.

According to research found by Enough is Enough, an organization whose mission is to make the internet safe for children and families, every minute, 63,992 new visitors arrive at Pornhub. Also, millennials, aged 18 to 34 remained the largest group to visit porn sites, with 61% of Pornhub's traffic. It's also alarming that the United States is a top consumer of both illegal child and obscene pornography.[6]

Shockingly, research studies by Covenant Eyes (an organization aiming at combating internet addictions), reveal that 11 is the average age that a child is first exposed to porn, and 94% of children will see porn by age 14. Additionally, 68% of church-going men and over 50% of pastors view porn on a regular basis. Pornography has not only invaded our overly sexualized culture, but it has unfortunately also invaded our churches.

It's no doubt that pornography distorts our perception of sexual intimacy and clouds our minds. However, the most damaging consequence is that it has the ability to threaten our salvation. Throughout the Scriptures, the Bible teaches us to run from sexual immorality and steer away from all manner of fornication and uncleanness. And for people who think that porn is only a male issue, let me tell you that it's not. It's a sin issue sponsored by the lust of the eyes. Surveys and research show that there's a growing number of women struggling with online porn. Beggar's Daughter, a website helping women to be set free from the porn lifestyle, shared that 87% of Christian women have seen pornography at some point in their lives. Lust certainly doesn't discriminate.

After repeatedly being exposed to pornographic materials, I started being tormented by the spirit of lust, day and night. My mind became the enemy's playground. I was regularly bombarded by sexual images and didn't know how to be set free. It was so destructive that I contemplated suicide on several occasions. I wanted to end this constant cycle of guilt, shame, and self-hatred. You need to understand that the enemy's plan is to kill, steal our destiny, and destroy our lives.

But thank God, in His infinite mercy, He set me free. He delivered me and gave me a new identity. That's the power of the love of God working within us. You don't have to live life in bondage. You can be set free by the power of the love of God. Regardless of the sin plaguing your soul, I believe that freedom and deliverance are available for each person.

God's love encountered me at the age of 18 years old. I was invited into a powerful church service, and for the first time, I experienced the tangible presence of God. I had never heard the message of salvation presented in that manner before. I didn't know that God actually wanted a personal relationship with me. I didn't feel worthy or even qualified to be embraced by Him. I felt dirty and not deserving of love. I was a dirty virgin, and He's always been a Holy God and a loving Father, pursuing me. His love pursued me from day one. From my mother's womb, He was relentlessly loving me. That's unconditional love.

Since then, I've been on a journey of applying the word of God to renew my mind. I began to grow in my understanding of my new identity as a daughter of the living God. My deliverance process did not happen overnight. I would speak the word of God over my mind and declare boldly everything that the Lord was speaking over me. I started memorizing the Scriptures and would intentionally recite them throughout the day. Step by step, I was challenging the lies of the enemies, and these sexual images slowly began to fade away. I became highly involved in church and ministry and built a community of mature believers around me. I was on my way to being totally delivered and set free from this addiction.

Looking back at my journey, it's apparent that the enemy tricks us into believing that we are not sinning simply because we may not be out there fornicating or we are not doing "the big sins." Then we come to the conclusion that we must be ok with God. Just because we are sinning differently or because our sins don't appear outwardly, doesn't mean that we are right with God. Back then, in my mind, I was glorifying the fact that I was a virgin and that my sins weren't as bad as other people's. That was pride talking for sure.

In my heart, I was justifying the reasons why my sins of indulging in pornography weren't as distasteful as the sins of those who were having sex outside of marriage. At least I wasn't out there giving my body to some guy who didn't love me nor value me. Those were the thoughts running through my mind at the time. Yes, I was very judgmental and self-righteous. How often do we judge others because they sin differently than we do? Sin is sin. There's no such thing as small, medium, or large sin.

The Scriptures tell us in Romans 3:23, that we've all fallen short of the honor and glory of God. No one is able to live a life that is pleasing to our Heavenly Father apart from the loving sacrifice that Jesus has done on the cross for us. I don't know about you, but the salvation message never gets old for me. May we never become disconnected from the truth that has set us free. My prayer is that we would often keep the image of the cross before our eyes and remind ourselves that it was God's unconditional love that propelled Jesus to the cross.

Has my life been sin-free from the moment I gave my life to Jesus? Of course not. It took years to break the cycle of bondage and pain that I was entangled in. However, my heart was repentant and turned towards the Lord. I was in constant pursuit of God. I was smitten by the love of God and growing as a redeemed daughter of God.

Author and Speaker, Jason L. Clark shared a powerful definition of what true repentance is on one of his social media posts:

"I'm seeing lots of calls and challenges online to repent. Yes, repent. Change the way you think until righteousness, peace, and joy are your reality. Until the confidence of on earth as it is in heaven is your perspective; until you sense the arms of your kind and loving Father enveloping you and you grow sure in His nature to work all things to our good. Repenting is not an act of desperation. It's not about begging or groveling for some reprieve or stay of execution from a judgmental God who is angry with us. He's not angry. He's in a good mood. His love is still the answer, is still measureless and true. Repenting isn't a heavy burden, a 24-hour wailing session focused on our brokenness and sin. Repenting is a 2 min, 4 min, 24 min, 24 hours or 240 days and on and on revelation of our Father's perspective in wish we lay our burdens down and exchange our brokenness for His righteousness, peace and joy.

Repenting is the gift that Jesus gave us to live as confident as sons and daughters in His love on earth as it is in Heaven."

I thank God that in His mercy, not only He delivered me, but also He ministered to me. As I matured in my walk with God, He told me that my virginity didn't impress Him. I hadn't realized that I was apparently wearing my virginity as a badge of honor. I was totally proud of it.

My reason for abstaining from sex was not necessarily that I wanted to honor God with my body. That was a secondary reason. I later found out when God convicted me that I was trying to prove that I was capable of following moral standards while others were not. Ouch! It's painful when God reveals the real motives and intentions of our hearts. But, only a loving Father can convict us in a powerful way that draws us closer to His embrace.

God's not moved by your virginity or celibacy (if you're in either category); He is after something greater. God wants us to be holy and pure. Holiness is greater than our decisions to stay celibate. Virginity and celibacy are mere fruits of a life of purity. Jesus didn't die for you to just be a virgin or celibate. Jesus died to reconcile us to the Father. He sacrificed everything so we can boldly take our rightful positions as sons and daughters of the Most High God.

Holiness is about stripping anything that displeases God and moving step by step closer to who He is. Holiness encompasses the intentions and motives of our hearts. You know that sometimes we don't always think clean thoughts, or we may not always have the right motives behind our actions. Holiness is deeper than us closing our legs and begging God to bring that man before we burn in our sins. Holiness is longing for everything God desires and hating everything He hates. There is an innocence in being pure before God, in our thoughts, our intentions, our hearts, and our actions. God wants our whole being to glorify Him. The closer we walk with God, the more we take on His nature so we can become more like Jesus Christ. God doesn't want us to have a form of Godliness; He wants us to be pure and holy.

God wants us to embrace holiness and purity as a lifestyle. Purity attracts the presence of God, His favor, and His blessings. God wants us to resemble the image of our savior Jesus Christ, who is the ultimate perfection of purity and holiness. I don't believe that we will attain complete purity on this side of Heaven, but the Word of God tells us that we can be holy as Christ is holy. Purity is a progressive process of allowing the Holy Spirit to refine and mold us on the Potter's wheel. A.W. Tozer beautifully said, *"our identification with Christ should be that whatever He is we also want to become."* In other words, everything that Christ is, we are. The truth remains that Jesus didn't just die for our forgiveness; He died to set us completely free.

God Kept Me

The grace to be kept in a society that unapologetically promotes sexual activity and promiscuity is available. At 35 years old today - by the grace of God - I'm still a virgin. I'm grateful, even though the journey has been challenging, God still kept me. I don't profess to have been an innocent person. I've put myself in compromising situations when I clearly knew that I had no business being alone with the opposite sex in apartments or cars. I was pretty foolish in my younger years.

Years ago, I got sexually assaulted by a boyfriend who took advantage of me and violently ripped my shirt off. He was 6'4, very muscular, and obviously a lot stronger than me. I don't know how I managed to escape that situation. All I know is, I was kicking my hands and legs as hard as I could. I must have screamed from the top of my lungs for him to stop. All I remember is quickly gathering my belongings and rushing to my car in disbelief. I never intended to end up in that situation. All I was looking for was his embrace. I didn't want to have sex. I wanted to be loved. I wanted to be affirmed. That's all I was looking for. Instead, I was violated and taken advantage of.

A Note to Those Who Choose Celibacy

Celibacy is not easy. I get it. But it's possible. God can keep you if you genuinely desire to be kept. In a culture that is oversaturated with sexual imagery, I can understand that it's not easy, but the truth remains, that you can be kept. Continue to honor God with your body, and one day, you will enjoy the beauty of intimacy with your spouse. Don't trust your flesh. It's easy to fall. I would encourage you not to flirt with the fire. There's a reason why the Scriptures remind us to flee from sexual sins.

Don't think that you're strong enough to withstand the temptations. RUN into your Heavenly Father's loving embrace. In that place of worship, you will find renewed strength, hope, and security. Our heavenly Father has provided us everything we need to live a godly life. Try not to put yourself in uncompromising situations. Set boundaries in your relationships. Invest time in the Word of God and in His presence. Feed your spirit and starve your flesh. Journal if you need to, as writing can be a very therapeutic exercise. Get productive and invest in your gifts. Go out there in the world; volunteer or try a new hobby. Whatever you do, live life to the fullest. We're only given now. Moment by moment is all we have. Trust God with your now and your tomorrow. He has kept you thus far, and He will never fail you.

The Highest Bride Price

In the African culture, when a woman is ready to be married, there are a series of festivities and celebrations that take place. Typically, there is a traditional ceremony that takes place before the white wedding. At the traditional event, the groom's family presents a variety of gifts, payments, or a mixture of both to the bride's family. In a lot of cultures around the world, this practice is known as the bride price. It's a symbolic, cultural custom that has been instituted for generations. In our modern era, families of African descent have modified the practice to their liking. Sometimes the bride's family will agree to "re-gift" the payments to the new couple.

Historically, the bride price pre-dates our financial system of cash. Back in the day, the bride price included gifts such as clothes, livestock (typically cows and goats), jewelry, and bottles of beer. The practice of the bride price is widely misunderstood by Westerners. This is not a tradition to "purchase" the bride or to encourage value to be placed on the material accomplishments of the bride-to-be. It's a bridal gift that serves as an opportunity for the husband's family to honor the family of his future in-laws.

Traditionally, when the bride price is received by the bride's family, the bride becomes one with her husband. When the bride price is presented to the bride's family, the bride disconnects from her father's house and now officially becomes a part of her husband's family. She then becomes the sole responsibility of her husband. At that moment, even though the Church wedding hasn't happened yet, the couple is considered to be married traditionally. From then on, It's understood that the groom is fully responsible to care for the bride, protect, and provide for her.

Now in the culture of the Kingdom of God, The Bible says that the Church is the bride and Jesus Christ is the bridegroom. For us to be married to Jesus Christ, He had to pay a bride price to release us from the bondage of sin. Sin demanded a high ransom that we couldn't satisfy. There's nothing that we could have done to bring about our own deliverance and freedom. Jesus paid the highest price for you and I. Once you accept that highest price that was paid for you, you are no longer your own. You now belong to the groom, Jesus Christ. At that point, you take on the groom's identity. He gave His blood that represents the highest bride price for us to walk in freedom, to know our identity, and to walk in our inheritance. Walking in our inheritance means fully receiving the fullness of who Christ is. That means to fully be conformed to His image and character.

For those who are struggling with your confidence, identity, and self-worth, I would like to encourage you to fully receive the love of God in your hearts. 1 John 4:18 tells us that, *"perfect love casts out all fear."* Amen. When the Love of God is perfected in you, it confronts all fears, all insecurities, all self-doubts, and the lies that you are not good enough, or you are not qualified or not worthy... All of those things dissipate when you understand that Christ paid

61

the highest bride price for you to know your identity and to walk in the fullness of your inheritance. Your self-worth is rooted in the Blood of Jesus Christ. The blood of Jesus gives us access to Jesus' identity, to His nature, and to His name.

When you understand that you were bought at the highest price, you will no longer be ashamed of your past. Your mistakes can no longer define you. You will no longer base your value on what people think of you. You could have been the prostitute down the street, but when you come to Christ, He applies His blood that gives you access to your birthright.

Your birthright represents your identity in Christ Jesus. We are born of the Spirit, so we are sons of God and co-heir with Jesus Christ. We've been given the right to call God, Abba Father. We will talk more about our identity as true sons and daughters in Chapter 5, *"Identity of True Sons and Daughters."*

Let me reiterate this so we understand the heavy investment that God deposited in each of us while we were yet sinners.

The Gift of Grace

The Holy Spirit reminded me of the scriptures in Romans, chapter 5, which explains that sin entered the world through Adam, and we were therefore alienated and utterly separated from God. However, Jesus Christ, who is God's perfect gift, was His redemptive plan for humanity. Simply put, God sent the second Adam to reconcile us to himself.

> *"For if, by the trespass of the one man (Adam), death reigned through that one man, how much more will those who receive God's abundant provision of grace and of the gift of righteousness reign in life through the one man, Jesus Christ!" Romans 5:17*

When I look back at my life, there have been times when I definitely didn't think I deserved God's grace, but He was still ever faithful to extend his forgiving hand and give me grace. God's forgiving nature blows my mind.

His ability to look at our sinful life and still forgive us every time we confess our sins often brings me to tears.

As humans, when someone offends us and hurts us, we are never quick to forgive. Our tendency is to hold grudges and rehearse the offense in our minds, over and over again. That's the truth. How many of us quickly forgive when someone hurts us? Thankfully, we have a God who is slow to anger and quick to forgive when we sin against Him. What's amazing is that He just doesn't stop there! The Bible reminds us that God removes our sins as far as the East from the West and never brings them up again (Psalm 103:12). God throws our sins into the sea of forgetfulness—when we confess them. That's grace.

I also need to point out, though, that grace is not a license to continue to sin. When we have a false understanding of the grace of God, we abuse it. Grace doesn't excuse repentance. God releases grace upon our lives when there's an evident heart transformation; when we've learned from our mistakes, and choose to live life His way. A repentant heart is a catalyst of God's grace. Grace is simply an opportunity to get it right. A second chance to get right with God.

God didn't have to forgive us, but He did. Simply because He loves us deeply and is interested in continuously growing a personal relationship with us as we become His sons and daughters. God is a forgiving Father, and he takes pleasure in restoring our lives the moment we humble ourselves before Him and acknowledge our sins.

Some of us are not proud of our past, and sometimes we look back down memory lane with regrets. Whatever your past looks like, the reality is that it could have been worse. Even in our disobedience, as we chose our own paths, God's unfailing love still kept us from digging deeper pits for ourselves. Instead of allowing regret's sorrowful grip to hold us captive to our past, let's begin to praise God for what He rescued us from. God is a God of the second chance, the fifth and the tenth chances; the one who gives us a clean slate when we repent and confess our sins.

"If we confess our sins to Him, He is faithful and just to forgive us and to cleanse us from all unrighteousness." 1 John 1:9

God is a Master Painter. He can take our doodling and with just a few strokes of His brush; He can create a masterpiece out of our mess. He takes flawed human beings and removes the sting of sin when we repent. And I truly believe that there is no human being that is so far removed from God's grace. His grace is available to all of us. The God of the second chance will not relent in pursuing us even when we fall or disappoint Him.

"God saved you by his grace when you believed. And you can't take credit for this; it is a gift from God." Ephesians 2:8

Where would we be without the grace of God? May the grace of God continue to draw us to a deeper fellowship with Him.

Chosen For His Purpose

God is the only one who can mend our broken hearts. Jesus didn't come for those who are well; He came to heal those who are broken. The Savior of the world came for those who have a less than perfect track record. Those who would be totally ashamed if a movie of their pasts or thought-life was on display for all to see. Christ came for the drunkards on the street, for the person living a double life and looking for a way out.

"You didn't choose Me, but I chose you and appointed you so that you should go and bear fruit, and that your fruit should remain." John 15:16

God doesn't choose you based on your performance, your beauty, your talents, or your tendency for perfection. Perfection doesn't move God. It's not about doing everything right that He may notice you and bless you. God simply chooses you; he called you because of the finished work that Jesus did on the cross. He nailed your sins to the cross when Jesus said, *"it's finished."*

Oftentimes, we can disqualify ourselves in so many ways; our accusing thoughts get the best of us. You may think that you are not qualified because you didn't pursue that higher education or you are not comfortable with public speaking. Can I tell you that God has a history of picking the ones that society rejected or the ones who believe they are not valuable enough?

Because of all these negative thoughts, we can sabotage God's work in our lives. Sometimes, we are our greatest obstacle. Our minds can be a place of defeat, but you can change that by rehearsing all that God says about you. The reality is that you will act on what you believe about yourself. What are you speaking over your life? What do you choose to agree with?

Here's the solution we all need. Take the word of God today and rehearse it. **Speak the truth of the word over your mind.** Declare today that you are the righteousness of God in Christ Jesus. Even though you've made mistakes in the past, God doesn't call you by your past. You are no longer called abused or rejected. You are Kings and Queens. You are God's son and daughter.

You can choose today to conform to the mind of Christ, and therefore, declare that you are accepted, called, chosen, and destined for success. You have great abilities and aptitudes because God doesn't create failures; everything He creates has life and potential to bear fruits. You are a seed from His mouth. When He spoke your name into existence, He also spoke substance and fruitfulness. You were made for signs and wonders. You were created for a divine purpose.

So the next time God calls you to a particular task or assignment, remember whose you are. If you need to start that new career, or open that orphanage, or start a foundation - whatever it is that God has placed on your heart, - know that you belong to God and that He is for you, so no one can be against you.

Break Every Chain

The Holy Spirit once showed me a profound picture that I can still see in my spirit. The room was pitch dark and there was no audible sound. In the middle of the room, was a man looking to the sky. The intensity of his eyes was the only thing illuminating the obscure jail cell he was confined to. The way he was looking up was as if he was expecting someone to rescue him from this dark abyss. But he was alone - completely barricaded by iron bars and unable to get out. As I saw his eyes again in the Spirit, I felt that he's been dealing with demons tormenting his mind for a very long time. He was mentally and emotionally drained and had no idea where his help would come from. I saw a man who was tired of his own sins, tired of the destructive cycle he found himself in. The more I saw him, the more I felt the pain of his broken pieces.

This man was in limbo. I felt that he was ready to surrender to Jesus, yet, the pride of life had him bound at the ankle. The lust of the flesh still felt good, so he was uncertain of his decision to follow Christ. Deep in my spirit, I was rooting for this man, believing that he would realize the danger of gaining the whole world and losing his soul (Mark 8:36). How I hope that he will surrender his broken pieces to God and allow his Heavenly Father to transform him with the only truth that will set him free.

Whether you're away from God, know God, or backslidden, there is power in the name of Jesus to break every chain - chains of pride, addiction, lust, depression, envy, anger, you name it.

Jesus is the Chain Breaker. He paid the highest bride price for your freedom through sonship.

Prophetic Declaration

You Love Me

Your love is my hiding place
Totally surrendered to your embrace
In You, I finally breath
I can let go now
I can stop striving
And fully be present
I'm yearning for that freedom to simply be

I surrender. Today. Tomorrow. For all eternity

The consistency of your love anchors me
You love me even when I fail to reciprocate
You love me through my ups and downs
You love me through my frustrations
You love me for me
Not a false version of me

In my humanity
In my frailty
In my questioning
In my anger
You love me

You wrap your arms around me and speak to my insecurities
You whisper in my ears that I'm forever Yours
Your presence is all I live for

Lord make me the vessel You desire me to be
Refine me and show me the meaning of life
Your love is the reason for being

4

The Father's Heart

As we embark on this chapter, there are some questions I would like us to ponder. I'd like us to take a moment to meditate on these and see what thoughts come to mind. Take your time to think through each of these questions, and no worries, relax, there are no tricky questions.

As we progress through this chapter, we're going to explore and unpack some of the themes revealed through these questions.

- Is God the object of your desire?
- Is improving your relationship with God at the top of your priorities?
- What characteristics of God's personality have you witnessed the most in your life?
- How would you define your journey with God up to this point?
- How involved is God in your decision-making?
- Is your relationship with God limited to a Sunday experience?

I've found that our responses to some of these questions reveal the quality of our relationship with God. Regardless of where you are in your knowledge and understanding of God, there's always more of Him to know. An intimate relationship with our Heavenly Father is **available** and **accessible** to anyone who surrenders their life to the Lordship of Christ. I truly believe that we have the ability to determine how close we want our relationship with God to be. As you draw near to God, He will draw near to you. God is eager to reveal Himself to us.

The truth of the matter is that God has always been pursuing us. We aren't the ones who made the first step. He extended an invitation to us before we even knew of Him. God has lavished his affection upon us from the very beginning of our existence. The Scriptures declare that God first loved us and intimately knew us before we were even in our mother's womb. God spoke to the prophet Jeremiah and told him:

> *"Before I formed you in the womb I knew you [and approved of you as My chosen instrument], And before you were born I consecrated you [to Myself as My own]; I have appointed you as a prophet to the nations."* Jeremiah 1:4-5 (AMP)

If God knew the prophet Jeremiah before he was even conceived, God knew you as well. Let me take it a step further and declare that I believe that God knew us intimately because we were in His loins (figuratively speaking) before the foundation of the world. When the Triune Godhead got together before the beginning of time, we were already in God's thoughts when He made Adam. It's a comforting reality to understand that God foreknew us and foreordained our lives to be molded into the likeness of His son, Jesus Christ. God's plan for each human soul is to encounter Him and to live in Him. God desires no one to perish. He wants each of us to come to a great awareness of His saving grace. God predestined us to a life of intimacy with Him. However, we've been given free will to decide whether to choose God's ways or not. In this fallen world, many decide to pursue their own will, and therefore, fall prey to the hands of Satan and his cohorts.

God has a plan and unique purpose for every soul that is born into this world. In fact, God called us to a higher calling in Him, not based on our merit, but to further His purpose, which was already given to each of us through Jesus Christ before the world began (2 Timothy 1:9). Before we were even born and had any knowledge of God, He had already made provision for the completion of our calling. Wow. How amazing is that truth!

God is a Master Planner whose intentions and plans for us are good. He strategically handpicked the work that He has called each of us to before the foundation of the world. The level of details that God orchestrates regarding our lives is simply mind-blowing. Not only did God know us intimately and intricately before we were even a thought, He knew the paths that we would take and the vocation that would exactly fit our make-up and personality.

I believe that He's constantly wooing us. His love is relentlessly pursuing us, but many haven't come to the realization that an intimate relationship with God is by far the most valuable aspect of our lives. Yes, God should be the most important relationship we pursue. It humbles me that the Creator of the universe, the One who formed the galaxies, stars, and planets, actually is interested in intimately walking with us. Think about it, there are billions of human beings on this planet, and yet, God knows their DNAs, names, addresses, occupations, dreams, and aspirations. He knows us deeply, but the question is, do we desire to know Him? Do we have an awareness of His presence? Is God at the center of our personal universe?

The most important thing we need to realize is that we can do nothing of eternal value without the presence of God. The sad reality is that many people who have some type of relationship with God have what I would like to call a "transactional relationship". In other words, there's an exchange that takes place between us and God. See, some people approach God only when they have a need, or when there's an emergency that arises, and they need God to intervene on their behalf.

With a transactional relationship, there's no intimacy or close friendship. There's only a superficial connection. You bring your need, and your expectation is that God would respond favorably and grant you the desires of your heart. Many people have a faulty perspective that God is a genie and that His responsibility is to respond to our demands. That's not how it works. We forget to understand that we were created to worship God, and it's not the other way around. We were created by God and for God. Your very existence is designed to glorify God from the breath you take every morning to the fulfillment of your projects and accomplishments. Your ultimate purpose here on earth is to magnify God and point others to Him.

We can't treat God the way some folks treat us. You know folks who only come to you when they want something from you! When they need information, or when they need a favor from you, or when they need money, that's when all of the sudden, they remember you. Suddenly, they act a little bit nicer because they need a favor from you. That's essentially the definition of a transactional relationship, or some people would call it "friends with benefits." There's no invested interest in the actual persons; the connection only exists because of what people can gain from it.

God made a valuable investment in our lives through the sacrifice of His son, Jesus Christ. Every day, He continues to give to us in variable forms without requiring reciprocity. Every day presents opportunities for us to grow in our awareness of God.

I believe worship is one of the vehicles that enable us to encounter the heart of the Father. God reveals His nature through the atmosphere of worship so we have an opportunity to get to know Him on a deeper level. Worship is a lifestyle and a medium through which we can intimately commune with our heavenly Father.

> "God is a Spirit, and those who worship Him must worship in spirit and truth." John 4:24 (KJV)

In other words, the only way we can connect with our heavenly Father is through a spiritual experience, not through our carnal or fleshly nature. When our human spirit pursues after God's Holy Spirit in purity, sincerity, and adoration, we experience the true meaning of life—which is the essence of worship. God's Holy Spirit is "pneuma"- the life-giving Spirit, the very air we breathe, and the source of our existence.

Worship is an act of admiration and devotion that is practiced by every human being, whether we realize it or not. Even people who don't know the one true God still worship. One form of worship that many in our society adhere to is idolatry. Our culture has had many idols we've exalted over the centuries.

Idolatry is very much alive today, and it's consuming our lives. Anything that we exalt above the knowledge of God becomes a counterfeit "god." Idols are designed to steal the worship that God deserves and ultimately seek to blind our spiritual eyes and lead us astray. Anything in our lives that is elevated at the same level of importance as our relationship with God, is an idol. In our current generation, it could be anything from smartphone addiction to our need to constantly check social media as if it was a drug.

Idolatry could also be evident in our unhealthy pursuit of money and material things or through our distorted allegiance to our political parties. Anything that disproportionately consumes your thinking and actions is an idol. For many, work and their unrestrained drive for success have led them to put God on the back burner. For others, it's their constant need to get approval from the influential people they respect the most.

I believe idols keep us from intimately knowing our Heavenly Father. It's our Father's desire to reveal Himself to us and make himself known. Idolatry is not only a concept of our current generation. In Ancient times, the Apostle Paul also highlighted the same concern. Let's look at the Scriptures below to gain deeper insight.

"So Paul, standing in the center of the Areopagus, said, "Men of Athens, I observe [with every turn I make throughout the city] that you are very religious and devout in all respects. Now as I was going along and carefully looking at your objects of worship, I came to an altar with this inscription: 'To An Unknown God.' Therefore what you already worship as unknown, this I proclaim to you: The God who created the world and everything in it, since He is Lord of heaven and earth, does not dwell in temples made with hands; nor is He served by human hands, as though He needed anything, because it is He who gives to all [people] life and breath and all things. And He made from one man every nation of mankind to live on the face of the earth, having determined their appointed times and the boundaries of their lands and territories. This was so that they would seek God, if perhaps they might grasp for Him and find Him, though He

is not far from each one of us." Acts 17:22-27 (AMPC)

In this passage of Scriptures, Paul is in Athens, more specifically in Areopagus, a place of great religious and philosophical influence. People would gather in the center of the city to engage in debates and introduce new concepts and ideologies. Athens was known for its pagan beliefs and its worship of Greco-Roman deities. In Acts 17, a group of philosophers began to argue with Paul and challenged his beliefs. That's when Paul saw an opportunity to share about the One true God who wants to make Himself known to all mankind. God doesn't want to remain unknown or relegated to a mystery personality. It's apparent that the Athenians understand the value of worship as we all were created to worship something. However, they were spiritually blind despite the level of intellectualism they operated in. Paul emphasized the truth of the Gospel that God wants us to know Him. I absolutely love how Paul highlighted the reality of God's **proximity** to each of us. God is so close to each of us. He's the very source of our lives and existence. According to John 17:3, Jesus tells us that knowing the Father and knowing him is the only way to experience eternal life. In other words, **God is very intentional in making Himself known by us.**

God is not just our maker, He's a loving Father, who is attentive to the joys and cries of His children. He's not removed from our day-to-day life, He's present and intentionally seeking intimate friendship with us. The Father's heart is for true communion with His children, partnering with us daily to advance His Kingdom agenda. God delights in doing life with us, the Bible tells us that He rejoices over us with gladness (Zephaniah 3:17).

Walking With God

This is an invitation to embrace the lifestyle of a true worshipper because there is always more of God to pursue. God gave His Son, Jesus Christ, for you and me, because he desires an unbroken friendship.

Recently, someone asked me where my passion for God originated from?

I smiled as I remembered my first encounter with Him. Years ago, when I invited Jesus into my heart, God's love truly transformed me. I couldn't deny that tangible encounter I had with Him. It was a precious experience that left me desiring more of God. There are some supernatural experiences that are hard to explain.

Since then, I've been pursuing God daily and intentionally. I enjoy being a carrier of His presence. As you invest in the pursuit of God, you will reap the benefits of serving Him. One of the most enjoyable benefits of seeking God is the proximity of walking with Him. As a loving Father, God wants an intimate friendship with His children.

Worship is a powerful conduit that enables us to know God more intimately. It's not a religious exercise, as some may believe; worship is a lifestyle of perpetual encounters with our Savior. Even when you've already committed your heart to Jesus, there is so much more of God beyond your salvation experience. Worship embodies your desire to pursue God. It improves the quality of our relationship with God, from acquaintances to best friends.

The lifestyle of worship exposes the attitude of our hearts. Because God reveals to redeem, He will uncover the condition of our hearts to heal us as we worship Him. There's a purification that takes place in the atmosphere of worship. When we stand in front of a Holy God, His presence burns the impurities of our hearts.

True worship is always God-centered. It's about desiring His presence and pursuing His face. So many people are seeking God's hands, always asking God for possessions and they come to Him with their endless list. Can we all put our lists aside for a moment and just seek His face?

When the Spirit of God dwells within you, you become His carrier. Everywhere you go, the Holy Spirit goes. Your worship experience can shift the atmosphere of any room or setting you step into. And do you know that even when you are working or doing anything as unto God, you are worshiping Him? When you do your job with excellence and your heart is turned toward God, you are worshiping Him! Your worship is an expression of God's glorious Spirit, who delights in revealing the essence of who God is.

When we intentionally and truthfully engage the Holy Spirit of God through the atmosphere of worship, we invite the character of God to invade our humanity. The reality of God's Kingdom is released through the purity of our hearts. Intimate worship is displayed in our **awareness** of God's sovereignty, through our ardent **availability,** and earnest **abandonment** to God's perfect will for our lives.

Let's look at two Bible characters whose lives I believe exemplified a lifestyle of worship.

Prophet Samuel

The story of the prophet Samuel, and the profound ways that God used him, are among my favorite Bible stories for multiple reasons. The circumstances surrounding Samuel's birth were a miraculous act of God's grace. In a time when the voice of God was rare in Israel and in the midst of uproars regarding nearby nations, Israel desperately needed a move of God. Spiritually speaking, the nation was in birth pangs as inhabitants needed to clearly hear God's voice and direction. Hannah (Samuel's mother) was barren for many years, believing that the Lord would open her womb and grant her heart's desires. The Lord blessing Hannah's womb was not just for her own benefit of childbearing, but it was also to usher the nation of Israel into a new era. A time when God's voice will again be sought after, and when the one true God will be revered and worshiped. In those days, even the priests and high priests were corrupt and were not living faithfully before the Lord. It amazes me that God always makes provision to redirect His people back to Him. His redemptive nature always creates a pathway that leads us back into the center of His heart.

Samuel was the ram that Israel needed.

"Elkanah knew Hannah, his wife, and the Lord remembered her. Hannah became pregnant and in due time bore a son and named him Samuel [heard of God], Because, she said, I have asked him of the Lord. And

Elkanah and all his house went up to offer to the Lord the yearly sacrifice and pay his vow.

*But Hannah did not go, for she said to her husband, I will not go until the child is weaned, and then I will bring him, **that he may appear before the Lord and remain there as long as he lives.***

*Elkanah her husband said to her, do what seems best to you. Wait until you have weaned him; only **may the Lord establish His word.** So Hannah remained and nursed her son until she weaned him.*

When she had weaned him, she took him with her, with a three-year-old bull, an ephah of flour, and a skin bottle of wine [to pour over the burnt offering for a sweet odor], and brought Samuel to the Lord's house in Shiloh. The child was growing.

Then they slew the bull, and brought the child to Eli.

Hannah said, Oh, my lord! As your soul lives, my lord, I am the woman who stood by you here praying to the Lord.

For this child I prayed, and the Lord has granted my petition made to Him.

Therefore I have given him to the Lord; as long as he lives he is given to the Lord. And they worshiped the Lord there. *1 Samuel 1:20-28* (AMPC)

From the very beginning, Samuel's life was set apart for the Lord as an offering of worship. His mother had dedicated him to the Lord as a sacrifice of worship and committed him to know the ways of God.

From a young age, he was discipled by Eli the High Priest, who taught Samuel how to minister before the Lord, serve in the tabernacle, and offer sacrifices on behalf of people. Clearly, God's hand was upon Samuel as he found favor both with God and man. The Lord had chosen Samuel as his faithful priest and prophet since he rejected Eli's sons (Hophni and Phinehas) for their immoral conduct and lack of reverence towards God.

Even though Samuel was under the mentorship and tutelage of Eli, he had a heart that was available and willing to yield to the Lord. In 1 Samuel 3, we see that God called Samuel on multiple occasions though he did not yet know the voice of God.

> *"And the Lord called Samuel the third time. And he went to Eli and said,*
> *Here I am, for you did call me. Then Eli perceived that the Lord was*
> *calling the boy.*
>
> *So Eli said to Samuel, Go, lie down. And if He calls you, you shall say,*
> *Speak, Lord, for Your servant is listening. So Samuel went and lay down*
> *in his place.*
>
> **And the Lord came and stood and called as at other times, Samuel!**
> **Samuel! Then Samuel answered, Speak, Lord, for Your servant is**
> **listening."** *1 Samuel 3:8-10*

When Samuel made himself available to the Lord and yielded to His voice, God charged Samuel with a prophetic message to release to the house of Eli. God was not pleased with the iniquity and the lack of restraint that Eli's sons were exhibiting. It's important to note that a heart of worship starts with a desire to make oneself completely available to God.

Availability is not just showing up. It's giving God undivided attention and devotion when you show up. It's being completely present and discerning of the things that God values the most. It's shutting off all manner of distractions and competing priorities so we can focus our gaze on the Lord.

I love that God was not hindered by Samuel's lack of awareness or understanding because he didn't yet have an encounter with the Lord. God saw Samuel's yielded heart and willingness to worship him. It takes a surrendered heart to yield to God's divine interruptions. The heart of the Father yearns for sons and daughters, who will welcome God's promptings and drop everything to tune into God's directives. That's the true heart of worship that God is after.

The Woman with the Alabaster box

Luke 7 highlights the story of a woman who invited herself to Simon's house while he was hosting a dinner party for Jesus.

> *"One of the Pharisees asked Jesus to dine with him, and He went into the Pharisee's house and reclined at table.*
>
> *And behold, a woman of the town who was an especially wicked sinner, when she learned that He was reclining at the table in the Pharisee's house, brought an alabaster flask of ointment (perfume).*
>
> *And standing behind Him at His feet weeping, she began to wet His feet with [her] tears; and she wiped them with the hair of her head and kissed His feet [affectionately] and anointed them with the ointment.*
>
> *Now when the Pharisee who had invited Him saw it, he said to himself, "If this Man were a prophet, He would surely know who and what sort of woman this is who is touching Him—for she is a notorious sinner (a social outcast, devoted to sin)."* Luke 7:36-50 *(AMPC)*

It's amazing how someone who is perceived as a social outcast and a notorious sinner can recognize the grace of God personified in Christ. Her love and admiration for Christ compelled her to weep at his feet, in worship. In the presence of the Messiah, the woman had an awareness of her immense need for forgiveness and grace. In her loving worship to the One who forgave and delivered her, she availed herself and poured out her most expensive sacrifice on Jesus' feet. She broke all societal protocols and didn't care about the opinions of those who were obviously judging her behavior.

This sinful woman anointed our Savior's feet in the house of Simon, the Pharisee, who had no revelation of the power of her act. People who are self-righteous like Simon, often have a low love reservoir for God because of their lack of discernment for how much God has forgiven them. True, intimate worship is born out of the sincerity of our yielded hearts.

My prayer for each of us is that we will grow in our awareness of God's presence through the lifestyle of intimate worship. As we're God's modern temple, His Holy Spirit is looking for willing vessels to abide in. As we continue to press into God's presence, we will become His conduits and vessels through which He can display His power and reach souls.

God wants us to cultivate His presence, and become carriers of His Spirit as we continue to mature as true sons and daughters.

Discerning The Voice Of The Father

Knowing God also means developing the ability to hear His voice. Yes, all of us are able to hear from the Lord regardless of how long we've walked with Him. Jesus points out in John 10:27 that His sheep hear His voice. In other words, God wants each of us to learn to discern and identify his voice. In order for us to know the voice of the Father, we have to experience the person of the Father through his Word. Knowing God starts with building a strong foundation of studying his Word.

> *"In the beginning was the Word, and the Word was with God, and the Word was God Himself. He was present originally with God. All things were made and came into existence through Him; and without Him was not even one thing made that has come into being. In Him was Life, and the Life was the Light of men." John 1:1-4 (AMPC)*

We understand from this passage, that before creation, Jesus was the Living Word who was not only with God, but he was also God from the very beginning of time. These scriptures not only reveal the Deity of our Lord Jesus Christ, but it also solidifies our Triune Godhead, as the Father, Son, and Holy Spirit. The Word, who was Christ from the beginning, became flesh and lived amongst us on the earth to lead us into a relationship with Father-God.

In the Word dwells the fullness of the meaning of life. It's impossible to know God apart from the Word, because the Word represents God. Every time we read God's Word, we receive life and have the opportunity to encounter Him. Intentionally engaging in reading God's word translates to making room for more of God's character and nature in our hearts. God's Word is the eternal way, the truth, the life, and the light that illuminates the souls of men. Because Jesus and the Father are one, we have been granted direct access to the Father through the vehicle of His Word.

> *"And this, **so that I may know Him** [experientially, becoming more* ***thoroughly acquainted with Him, understanding the remarkable*** ***wonders of His Person more completely***] *and [in that same way experience] the power of His resurrection [which overflows and is active in believers], and [that I may share] the fellowship of His sufferings, by being **continually conformed** [inwardly into His likeness even] to His death [dying as He did]..."* Philippians 3:10 (AMP)

I don't believe it's possible to know God intimately without the discipline and commitment of studying His word. The Word of God is not an ancient or outdated book of wisdom and parables. It's a living, God-breathed, and inspired book that reveals the heart and mind of God and gives us a glimpse into the loving, just, and redemptive character of our Heavenly Father. The Word of God has the ability to transform us into the image and likeness of Christ when we allow it access into our minds, emotions, experiences, and hearts. In fact, Hebrews 4:12 declares:

> *"For the Word that God speaks is alive and full of power [making it active, operative, energizing, and effective]; it is sharper than any two-edged sword, penetrating to the dividing line of the breath of life (soul) and [the immortal] spirit, and of joints and marrow [of the deepest parts of our nature], exposing and sifting and analyzing and judging the very thoughts and purposes of the heart."* Hebrews 4:12 (AMPC)

The Word of God has the ability to discern our hearts' intentions and motives while providing a pathway for transformation, so we can become incrementally more like our great High Priest, Jesus Christ.

God has given each of us the ability not just to know Him through His Word, but also to hear His voice. You don't have to operate in the five-fold ministry graces to hear the voice of God. In other words, you don't need to be in any leadership role or have any titles to hear God's voice. Our Heavenly Father is eager to communicate with you. Whether you're just starting out your walk with Him or you've been a believer for some time, our Heavenly Father is inviting us to know His voice.

In the midst of a chaotic world, in which we're bombarded by so many people's opinions and perspectives, it's imperative that we cultivate the ability to keenly discern the voice of God. It's easy to be overwhelmed by the voice of the media that propagates fear, confusion, and division, or the voices of our culture that promote consumerism and pressure us to compare our lifestyles to others, only to make us miserable when we listen to its lies.

Psychologists believe that a person's voice reveals a great deal about their personalities and overall life experiences. A person's voice can sometimes convey confidence or can also reveal areas of insecurity or uncertainty. Your voice identifies your uniqueness to the world and highlights your authenticity. Your voice doesn't just encompass elements such as your pitch, tone, volume, diction, or the rhythm of your intonation. A person's voice is a lot deeper than the sound that is projected from their mouth. Your voice is rooted in your belief system and is a combination of the values you uphold, the thoughts that you meditate on, your daily attitude, and your disposition towards life. Whether metaphorically or literally speaking, a person's voice always points to their identity. What does your voice reveal about you?

As we continue to grow in our friendship with the Lord, we will be able to clearly discern God's character and intentions through His voice. God's voice is not ambiguous; it's clear and always unveils His heart towards us. God is consistently communicating with His children, if we can slow down long enough to tune in to His voice. God's voice, echoed in the Scriptures, introduces us to His love, mercy, peace, righteousness, justice, and grace that can only be found through the free gift of Salvation. The Word clearly tells us that in the past generations, God has predominantly spoken through our forefathers and the prophets; however, in our dispensation, God's voice is mainly communicating to us through the person of Jesus (Hebrews 1:1-2). In many ways, learning to distinguish the voice of God from other voices starts with our friendship and intimacy with Jesus. Let's look at the characteristics of these voices below and how they differ from the voice of our Heavenly Father.

Your Own Voice:

- Typically reveals the desires of your heart and the intentions of your mind.
- Has the ability to choose to worship God. (Psalm 30:12)
- Has the power to declare life and death over any situation. (Proverbs 18:21)
- It indicates your worldview and the opinions that you have on various matters.
- Has the ability to build, exhort, and encourage others. (Ephesians 4:29)
- Has the power to engage in spiritual warfare waged against the knowledge of God. (2 Corinthians 10:5)
- Often exposes your internal frustrations and disappointments of life.
- Enables you to engage in the fight for justice and stand up for the defenseless. (Proverbs 31:8-9)

Satan's Voice:

- Satan is the father of lies; he doesn't have the ability to tell the truth. His voice always reveals his deceptive nature. (John 8:44)
- His voice is always accusatory and condemning, always highlighting our faults and shortcomings. (Revelation 12:10)
- It's a voice that is often driven by rebellion, pride, and selfish ambitions.
- It's a voice of lack and deficit seeking to steal your joy, peace, and life. (John 10:10)

- Any word or any doctrine that is not in alignment with the Word of God is from the enemy.
- The devil always comes to distort the truth of God's Word.
- The voice of the enemy points to his shrewd and malicious character, seeking to devour his prey with his cunning words and tactics. (1 Peter 5:8)
- Satan's voice always sows fear and doubt into our hearts to discredit God's credibility and authority.
- The voice of the enemy causes us to doubt God's ability to perform His word. Doubt is a spirit that causes us to question the validity and relevance of God's Word.
- The enemy's voice is filled with confusion and always contradicts the message of the cross.

The Father's Voice:

- The voice of The Father will always be in agreement with His Word. The Holy Spirit will never speak anything that is contrary to God's written Word. (Romans 10:17)
- God's voice is a voice of reassurance and truth. God is not a man that He should lie, as the Word declares in Numbers 23:19, so His voice speaks of His integrity and reveals the consistency of His character over the generations.
- The voice of the Father is a voice of conviction and not condemnation. Conviction highlights sin and leads us to repentance. It's redemptive in nature, as it's designed to draw us closer to the Father. Condemnation, on the other hand, is a lie of the enemy, filled with guilt, seeking to drive a wedge between us and the Father.
- The voice of the Father always affirms your identity and speaks of your sonship. (Mark 1:11)
- The voice of God brings stillness to your soul. (Psalm 37:7)
- The voice of God anchors your emotions and heart in His goodness.

- The voice of the Father will never remind you of the guilt of your past sins; it will always point you to the finished work of the Cross.
- The voice of God speaks of His justice and enforces the preeminence of Christ. (Colossians 1:18)
- The voice of the Father leads us in the depth of His love, where there's an absence of fear. (1 John 4:18)

Understanding God's heart means that we need to fall in love with His word and learn to discern His voice from the adversary's voice. As we read the word of God and become more aware of how God speaks to us through His Word and the Holy Spirit, we will recognize the variance of God's tone within His voice. Ultimately, when we are acquainted with the heart of God, we'll know that when He speaks, it's always from a place of compassion and love regardless of how stern his tone sounds.

The Fruit of Discipline

Experiencing the discipline of God is one of the markings of a true son or daughter. God disciplines us, not necessarily because we've done something wrong, but because it's a crucial aspect of our training process. In order for us to fully identify with Christ's nature, we have to partake of the fullness of who He is - through His glorious power and His sufferings.

The discipline that suffering produces is a lifestyle of holiness, which creates an aroma that is pleasing to our Heavenly Father. Holiness is a fragrance that identifies us as God's sons and daughters. When God tests us, it's never with the intention of condemning us or severely reproving us. Our Heavenly Father is not out to get us or to pick apart our inadequacies or faults.

Some believers think that God is waiting for us to stumble so He can call down fire from Heaven and rejoice at our demise. Nope! That's definitely not the character of the God that we serve. God is passionately in love with each of us and is relentlessly pursuing us. He is far more invested in us and interested in our transformation journey. Through His unfailing love and holy nature, He made provision for our redemption and sanctification. That's how fierce and deep God's love is for us. His desire is to mature us into the likeness of His Son, Jesus Christ, as He perfects our faith through the trials and testings of life.

The problem that I've witnessed is that our Western ideologies have infiltrated our Christianity and created a belief system that is far from what the Bible actually teaches. Nobody talks about the sacrifices that are required of a true follower of Christ or the painful but yet necessary journey of dying to self. In our seeker-friendly culture, we emphasize the idea of coming to Jesus as you are, but very few focus on the radical change involved in growing as a follower of Christ.

Jesus didn't die for our sins so we can barely make it into the Kingdom of God. He died so we can experience the fullness of His nature through the gift of sonship and become one with our Heavenly Father. Hence, the Scriptures encourage us not to despise the chastening or the training of the Lord because of the eternal benefits that it produces.

Let's take a look at the Word, in Hebrews 12:5-11 to dig a little deeper:

"And have you [completely] forgotten the divine word of appeal and encouragement in which you are reasoned with and addressed as sons? My son, do not think lightly or scorn to submit to the correction and discipline of the Lord, nor lose courage and give up and faint when you are reproved or corrected by Him;

For the Lord corrects and disciplines everyone whom He loves, and He punishes, even scourges, every son whom He accepts and welcomes to His heart and cherishes.

You must submit to and endure [correction] for discipline; God is dealing with you as with sons. For what son is there whom his father does not [thus] train and correct and discipline?

Now if you are exempt from correction and left without discipline in which all [of God's children] share, then you are illegitimate offspring and not true sons [at all].

Moreover, we have had earthly fathers who disciplined us and we yielded [to them] and respected [them for training us]. Shall we not much more cheerfully submit to the Father of spirits and so [truly] live?

*For [our earthly fathers] disciplined us for only a short period of time and chastised us as seemed proper and good to them; but **He disciplines us for our certain good, that we may become sharers in His own holiness.***

*For the time being no discipline brings joy, but seems grievous and painful; but afterwards **it** yields a peaceable fruit of righteousness to those who have been trained by it [a harvest of fruit which consists in righteousness—in conformity to God's will in purpose, thought, and action, resulting in right living and right standing with God]." Hebrews 12:5-11 (AMPC)*

If Jesus, as the Son of the Living God, has been trained by the trials that He endured, why do we often think that we can bypass this process of maturation? We just read that the Scriptures tell us that all of God's children share this reality. In order to grow and become more Christ-like in our nature and character, we will be tested, pruned, and disciplined. Let's focus on the word "pruning" for a moment, as it is a very familiar word used in the Scriptures. In John 15:1-17, Jesus gives the disciples a powerful revelation about the purpose of pruning and the importance of abiding in Him. Jesus clearly addresses that our ability to grow and bear fruit in life is first determined by our ability to remain rooted in Him, as He is the true vine. In His gardening analogy, Jesus highlights the Father's responsibility in pruning branches that are already bearing fruits, so they can produce even more fruits. He further declares that our Heavenly Father is glorified in our fruit-bearing.

When we closely look at John 15, we quickly understand that pruning is a spiritual practice that our Heavenly Father takes us through. In the practical sense of the word, pruning is the practice of cutting off old wood as much as possible to allow the new wood to grow properly. Additionally, the pruning process involves the removal of non-productive, or damaged branches and stubs to position them to bear **better quality fruits**. Being more fruitful is not just about our ability to produce, but it also involves our capacity to yield **healthy fruits**. We can often become damaged branches yielding fruits that are not necessarily glorifying the Father.

In the gardening world, a pruning process is a yearly event that the gardener doesn't miss. For most vines and plants, pruning typically takes place during their dormancy, which is often towards the end of the winter months. A plant dormancy refers to its resting period and a time of preparation to transition to the upcoming season. It's during this time that the gardener takes time to repair the branches and train the stems that have become so tangled and weighed down. Just like plants and vines go through their dormant phase, I've come to understand that our ability to fully rest in Jesus has a tremendous impact on our productivity. Resting in God is a place in which we stop striving in our own human efforts and fully surrender to God's divine plan of action. It's God's plan executed through our lives that is designed to effectively advance His Kingdom. When we rest in Jesus and allow our Heavenly Father access to our hearts, our thoughts, and our dreams, He prunes the stems that have been tangled by worldly thinking so He can reposition us for massive Kingdom impact.

God's love and providence are the driving forces behind every season that He allows us to go through. God's heart in pruning and disciplining us is to save us from our carnal destructive nature. Left alone, our defiant behavior has the capacity to lead us astray and cause negative consequences in our lives. So God, out of love, provides ways to confront our strong will and orchestrate life's events that will cause us to get to the end of ourselves. God will often use the disappointments of life, and the delays or frustrations we experience to break us to a place of pliability. Our flesh is a strong-willed and independent agent that has no intention of willingly submitting to God's divine plan for our lives. You and I both know that the flesh has a mind of its own. It's adamant in its desire to do everything that is contrary to the desires of the Holy Spirit. That's why the Word declares that our flesh is enmity against God.

"[That is] because the mind of the flesh [with its carnal thoughts and purposes] is hostile to God, for it does not submit itself to God's Law; indeed it cannot." Romans 8:7 (AMPC)

The reality is that we can't please God if we have a propensity to live a fleshly lifestyle. We will always be in opposition with the Spirit of God when we don't live a yielded life. That's why many believers live in a constant internal tug of war because their flesh is stubborn as a mule. We can't wholeheartedly worship Jesus if we're married to our will. Either Jesus is the Captain of our ship or we are.

The discipline that the Lord orchestrates in our lives is designed to sanctify and refine our character, so we can produce the fruit of holiness. Without this fruit of holiness, the Scriptures say that no one can see the Lord.

"Strive to live in peace with everybody and pursue that consecration and holiness without which no one will [ever] see the Lord." Hebrews 12:14 (AMPC)

God is essentially preparing us, through the refining process, so He can present us holy and blameless to Himself.

Sometimes, the pride of our human spirit can only be weakened and broken through life's difficult events. God's purpose in crushing the arrogance of our carnal nature, is to unite us with His Holy Spirit. Oneness with the Holy Spirit can only occur with a pure and yielded vessel. Our obstinate, fleshly nature is perhaps one of the strongest hindrances to the move of the Holy Spirit in our lives.

When we've been broken by the trials of life, there's a deeper unification process that takes place with the Holy Spirit. We can only be useful to the Kingdom of God when we've been processed and our faith has been tested by fire. Our fleshly agenda will never advance the Kingdom of God. An agenda that is submitted to the Lordship of Christ is the only plan that has the capacity to advance the Kingdom of God.

It can be challenging to comprehend the beauty and benefit that discipline produces if we don't have a revelation of the Father's heart towards us. The breaking, the molding, and the pruning are all conspiring to grow the mature sons and daughters that creation is earning for. When we welcome the testing of God and fully submit to His will, not only will we produce the fruit of righteousness, but our faith also has an incredible opportunity to grow. Our ability to deeply trust God through the seasons of life that He takes us through, reveals the maturity of our sonship.

We were created to bear eternal fruits that glorify the Father and advance His Kingdom. Whether God is pruning us to address an entitlement mindset or to expose our self-righteousness, or complaining tendencies, His work in our life is very intentional. God's divine training disconnects us from unfruitful mindsets and thinking patterns that are not aligned with His nature. In order for us to continue to produce richer and excellent fruit that is evident through our thoughts, values, and actions, we've got to fully live immersed in Jesus, who is the true Vine. It's only in abiding in Christ, that the Father can perfect us into the likeness of His Son.

There's nothing more reassuring than trusting the God who spoke the universe into existence and holds billions of stars in place. There's no better place to be but in His perfect will. The Father desires deep intimacy and friendship with each of His children. He is calling us to a closer walk with Him, unhindered by the affairs of the world. The Father's heart is to continue to build us as His dwelling place, by living out His legacy and influence through our vessels. He's searching for hearts that will be willing to carry the true essence of who He is into every area of our culture. May we learn to delight in our Father's embrace and carry His name through the love we display for one another and through the purity of our worship.

5

Identity of True Sons & Daughters

"For you have not received a spirit of slavery leading again to fear [of God's judgment], but you have received the Spirit of adoption as sons [the Spirit producing sonship]." Romans 8:15 (AMP)

I've always been fascinated with the concept of identity. According to the Cambridge Dictionary, the noun **identity** is who a person is, or the qualities of a person or group that make them different from others. It encompasses information such as a person's name, date of birth, and other distinctive characteristics that set them apart from everyone else.

The American Psychological Association takes it deeper in defining the word identity. According to its dictionary, identity is an individual sense of self, defined by a set of physical, psychological, and interpersonal characteristics that is not wholly shared with any other person. Identity also involves a range of affiliations, ethnicity, social roles, and the feeling that one's memories, goals, values, expectations, and beliefs belong to the self.[7]

Our identity distinguishes us, revealing our uniqueness and authenticity. Every single one of us at one point or another has been in search of understanding who we are, where we come from, and what gives us value. We all yearn to be validated and desire for the world to accept our most authentic selves.

We all want to be celebrated, seen, and heard. That desire comes from our need to be significant, relevant, and accepted. Simply put, we all want to belong. Whether you're the CEO of a company, a teacher, scientist, or a janitor, we're all looking for someone to validate our identity. Some look to their parents, or maybe a mentor or a role model, who significantly impacted their lives. Others look for identity by belonging to a specific cultural or social group they define themselves by. It's no doubt that our identity is largely formed by the voices that shaped our upbringing, the belief systems dominant in our environment, and the choices we've made in life.

In biology, we've all learned that the gender identity of a child is highly dependent on the man. Men determine the sex of the baby based on what chromosome their sperm carries, whether X or Y. An X chromosome married to the mother's X will produce a baby girl. On the other hand, a Y chromosome, when combined with the mother's, makes a boy. It's fair to say that children's gender identity is largely decided by their biological fathers, even though we draw our characteristics and traits from the genes we inherit from both parents.

In my understanding of our Christian journey, it's apparent to me that the concept of identity is also an extremely important one. Our religious background, or sometimes the lack of it, often shapes our spiritual realities. Ultimately, questions such as, "Who am I?" and, "Where did I come from?" often demand a deeper answer. For many of us, when we started asking those questions, we weren't looking for superficial answers.

Unbeknownst to us, many of us were looking for a spiritual encounter. If our earthly parents have the ability to transfer traits that shape who we are as individuals, our Heavenly Father's influence in molding our lives is even greater. The Bible declares that we are God's masterpiece, crafted and fashioned in the image of God. From the womb, we were fearfully and wonderfully created in the likeness of God. God, who knows each of us so intimately, has intricately taken time to knit every single detail of our physical characteristics and personality traits and has also planted eternity in our hearts.

If you ever wonder why we yearn for something greater than life, it is because God has designed our soul to continually thirst for His presence. However, human beings over the generations have searched for ways to find purpose and fulfillment in worldly or material things. We can search high and low for a sense of identity and significance, but sooner or later, we all realize that God alone can satisfy us. His presence is the breath and fullness of life we're craving.

Purpose and Intentionality

I truly believe that you will never be satisfied with life until you know why you are here on earth. Life without purpose is simply meaningless. Purpose is what feeds your spirit and motivates you to fully live every day. Purpose ignites your soul and gives you the drive to persevere. The essence of who you were designed to be was deposited in you long before you were born. Believe it; it's in you. Purpose is not a course you can take in school as you pursue your career. Walking in your purpose is not something that can be taught. Purpose is already inside of you. It needs to be awakened. The awakening process starts the moment we decide to pursue God. It's only then that a beautiful discovery process begins to unfold.

Purpose is crucial and extremely essential. It's God's blueprint for your life. You just need to awaken to it and embrace it. It's that which God has called you to do here on the earth. The word says in Ephesians 2:10, *"For we are God's workmanship, created in Christ Jesus for good works, which God prepared beforehand that we should walk in them."* (NKJV) God has placed a seed of purpose in you. Every single one of us has something of value on the inside of us. As you pursue God, He will place a demand on that seed so it can produce life and bear fruits that others can benefit from.

Discovering your purpose and growing in it shouldn't be complicated. It seems like we've made the idea of purpose more complex than what God intended it to be. Your purpose is best displayed when God is using you in the unique way you were wired. Purpose is being where God wants you to be and doing the things He wants you to do moment by moment in your journey in life. Simply put, purpose is being in the center of God's will for your life.

I'm reminded of the word that Jesus shared in John 4:,

> *"My food is to do the will of Him who sent me and to finish His work."*
> *John 4:34 (NKJV)*

I love how Jesus chose to use the word "food" as an analogy to illustrate his point. Some Bible translations use the word "meat" instead of "food." This reference to something that we eat is powerful! Food gives us sustenance. It provides the minerals, vitamins, and the fuel we need physically and mentally to accomplish what the Lord has called us to do. In other words, Jesus was saying that my purpose, or the reason for my existence on the earth, is to please God and to do His will. In using the analogy of food, Jesus was also highlighting the source of his satisfaction. Jesus was publicly declaring that fulfilling the will and plan of God was the only thing capable of satisfying his hunger and zeal in life.

So, when we talk about purpose, we need to understand that it's not about us. Walking in your purpose is about using your gifts, talents, and resources to glorify God as you serve others. As a spiritual son or daughter, your purpose is bigger than your own aspirations.

Martin Luther King Jr, once prayed this prayer, *"Use me, God. Show me how to take who I am, who I want to be, and what I can do, and use it for a purpose greater than myself."* The purpose of our existence is connected to the assignment of God upon our lives. We need to understand that there are breakthroughs in people's lives that are dependent on our willingness to embrace and to walk in our purpose.

Within you lies an anointing to transform lives. Communities are waiting for you to fully walk in your purpose. It's about touching lives, mentoring people, providing guidance, and leaving a mark and a legacy for the generations to come.

Kingdom Purpose

As sons and daughters of God, we've inherited His Kingdom, His ways, and a great responsibility to further grow its influence. It's really the honor and privilege of our life to be called God's children and co-heirs to His promises. When we're grafted into the Kingdom of God through the sacrifice of our Lord and Saviour Jesus Christ, we then awaken to our Kingdom Purpose.

Apostle John Eckhardt declared in one of his sermons titled Apostolic Kingdom that *"the primary reason Jesus came to earth was to inaugurate the Kingdom of God. Often, we hear that the reason Jesus came to the earth was to die on the Cross. Jesus did come to die on the Cross, but that death on the Cross was for the purpose of establishing the Kingdom of God."*

Jesus' assignment on the earth was to establish the Kingdom of God. Our God-given purpose as his sons and daughters is to continue to further its influence in every region and sphere of our society. This is the beauty of our shared Kingdom purpose, as believers in Christ Jesus. We're ultimately called to the same purpose which is to glorify God and advance His Kingdom, however, the expression and the execution of that divine purpose look different for each of us. Some are called to influence the media industry, others are called to infiltrate the educational system with the truths of God's word. Other believers are commissioned to be salt and light in the marketplace while others are tasked to perform research studies in the scientific community.

Let's look at the Scriptures, in Colossians 1:13-14:

> *"[The Father] has delivered and drawn us to Himself out of the control and the dominion of darkness and has transferred us into the kingdom of the Son of His love, In Whom we have our redemption through His blood, [which means] the forgiveness of our sins." Colossians 1:13-14 (AMPC)*

This powerful Scripture encapsulates God's heart in birthing us into His Kingdom and it also gives us a synopsis of what the gospel is all about.

The Gospel is often referred to as the good news. The gospel essentially is the revelation of Jesus Christ through God's infallible Word. I believe that the gospel introduces us to the reality of our sonship when we receive the love of God. When we invite Jesus into our hearts, we're ushered into the Kingdom of God. We then become sons and daughters of the living God. God's original intent has always been intimacy and closeness with his children.

Becoming true sons and daughters of God means embracing the sacrifice that Jesus has done on the cross for the remissions of our sins. It also means receiving Christ as our personal Lord and not just our Savior and exchanging our lives for His. I believe that many believers haven't fully embraced the gift of sonship because of our hesitancy to surrender to Jesus as our Lord.

When Jesus becomes our Lord, we learn to fully submit every area of our lives to his leadership and His will. The reason why many believers are comfortable with Jesus being their Savior is that we think about salvation and we think mostly about the hope of eternal security. However, few give thoughts to the importance of giving Jesus access to the areas of our lives we "control."

Growing as a son and daughter of God will require that we relinquish control of our lives and fully give Jesus the permission to rearrange our lives according to His divine will. The idea of Jesus being our Lord reveals our ability (or lack thereof) to trust Him with the elements of our humanity. Give Christ permission to lead you in the area of your finances, in your relational decisions, or even in the business ventures you engage in. Our ability to continue to grow in the fullness of sonship largely depends on our willingness to let go of the need to control our lives.

In Chapter 3, we talked about the bride price, which is the highest price that was paid so you and I can enter into a relationship with our Heavenly Father. The bride price confirms our birthright, which is our identity. Our identity in Christ reveals our inheritance. We are partakers of Christ's identity and inheritance because of the bride price. Our inheritance as sons and daughters of God encompasses blessings, resources, and gifts.

In order for us to walk in the fullness of our Sonship in Christ, we also have to stop running away from the call of God upon our lives. I'm talking to believers, not unbelievers. Just because you're born again doesn't mean that you're walking in all that God has birthed you into the Kingdom for. I'd like to encourage you to completely commit to yield to God's plans for your life.

I sense that some of you are counting the cost of fully being dedicated to Christ. You rather have one foot in the world and one foot in God, in fear that this Jesus walk doesn't produce the life that you desire or requires too much from you. Let me tell you that yielding to Christ is worth it. It's about your life being a ministry tool in His hands. Being sold out to Christ is what will truly give meaning and significance to your life. Anything outside of faithfully serving God will only provide temporary relief or satisfaction.

At the end of the day, it's all about God's purposes manifesting here on the earth, as we discussed earlier. God is after total surrender; He's not satisfied with our partial devotion and flaky commitment to His will. Jesus didn't die on the cross so we could become part-time believers or lukewarm followers.

We need to get a revelation of the weight of the investment that God deposited in each of us when we got saved. It's time to place tremendous value on the calling of God upon your life. Quit looking at yourself as a second-class citizen because of your past or the things you're going through. It is God who has rescued us from the kingdom of darkness and birthed us into the Kingdom of Light so we can be a reflection of His son, Jesus Christ.

We are each called to leave an imprint on this Earth—an eternal legacy that will point others to Christ, even when we're gone. Your birth and presence on this earth is extremely strategic. There's a reason you were born for such a time as this, to live a life that ought to be greater than you. Your contribution to the world is not accidental. Part of walking in our inheritance as spiritual sons and daughters of God is understanding that our lives are filled with assignments and purposes beyond ourselves.

Have you ever seen the movie Hidden Figures? I thought it was an epic movie released back in 2016. Hidden Figures highlights the powerful story of three African-American mathematicians, who God used tremendously to bring about breakthroughs and major advancements in NASA. The movie depicts the story of Katherine Johnson (played by Taraji P. Henson), Dorothy Vaughan (as Octavia Spencer), and Mary Jackson (portrayed by actress Janelle Monae). This movie is based on a true story of women who were trailblazers and who rose up to the assignment of redefining societal norms. Their brilliant minds were instrumental in launching astronaut John Glenn into orbit in 1962.

These women were born at a specific time in history when segregation was still very much a part of their daily lives. Universities, libraries, and bathrooms were still separated between colored and whites. According to the article written by National Geographic entitled "Women in NASA," women played a crucial role in the United States space effort. African-American women were specifically vital in their roles in helping to advance NASA's mission. These women were highly intelligent "human computers" working on complex mathematical calculations and equations by hand.[8]

The women of NASA knew their assignments and were invested in doing their part to contribute to re-shaping history. These brilliant minds were strategically positioned by God in the right generation. In His infinite wisdom, God birthed these women in the right era in the midst of adversity, which will ultimately create the perfect sets of circumstances to reveal His purposes. God knew that it would take the resilient spirits of these women, their ingenious minds, and their personalities to challenge the status quo of their times. Change was imminent because these women set up and sacrificed their comfort to say 'yes' to a mission bigger than themselves.

We also learn from these inspiring women, that adversity is part of the equation in life. Everything that you're going through and everything that God allowed in our lives have a purpose. If we learn to manage adversity well, we'll understand that it is designed to make us stronger. Adversity is the very thing that God will use as a launchpad to propel us into our destiny.

The Kingdom Of God And Our Position In Christ

As sons and daughters of the Living God, it's imperative that we gain revelation of the Kingdom we were born into. We thank God for the gift of salvation that ushered us into His Kingdom. I'm reminded of the conversation that Jesus had with Nicodemus, who was a Pharisee and one of the rulers of the Jews. John 3 tells us that Nicodemus sought Jesus by night to visit with Him, as he was amazed by the miracles that Jesus performed. Jesus took that opportunity to emphasize the need for every man and woman to be born again in order to enter the Kingdom of God. Further in the conversation in John 3:16, Jesus makes things plain and introduces Nicodemus to the Gospel message that is the key needed to enter the Kingdom of God. The key is the good news of salvation, which opens the door to the Kingdom of God.

> *"I am the Door; anyone who enters in through Me will be saved (will live). He will come in and he will go out [freely], and will find pasture." John 10:9 (AMPC)*

As we're born of the Spirit, we're introduced to a Kingdom that is not from this world. The Kingdom of God is unlike any earthly kingdom. I believe that the Kingdom of God represents God's ruling in the hearts of those who recognize His sovereignty and surrender to His eternal authority. Additionally, Romans 14:17 further reveals that the foundation of the Kingdom of God is based upon righteousness, peace, and joy in the Holy Spirit.

In other words, the Kingdom of God is not about external factors like our appearances or preferences. The Kingdom of God is evidenced in a heart posture that is willingly submitted to the Lordship of Christ. This is a great reminder to us all that there's nothing about our spiritual experience with the Lord that is based on our external works. The Kingdom of God is a gift that is sponsored by God's amazing grace and the finished work of the Cross.

As sons and daughters of the Most High, we are given the opportunity to grow in our understanding of Christ and the Kingdom we've inherited. The Word declares in 2 Corinthians 5:20:

> *"So we are Christ's ambassadors, God making His appeal as it were through us. We [as Christ's personal representatives] beg you for His sake to lay hold of the divine favor [now offered you] and be reconciled*

to God." 2 Corinthians 5:20 (AMPC)

We are God's representatives and citizens of His Kingdom. We are His ambassadors on the Earth to represent the interest of the Kingdom of God. Our responsibility is to emulate the life of Jesus, rule, and reign through His authority, and dismantle the works of the devil. In politics, an ambassador is a high-ranking diplomat whose main assignment is to represent and defend the interests of their country of origin. They operate under the authority of the government they are from and not under the host nation. As a representative of their country, they enforce the culture, viewpoints, and platforms of their home country's President. Ambassadors are provided for, well protected, and properly resourced by the regime that they represent.

Likewise, our responsibility as Kingdom ambassadors is to represent the affairs of the Kingdom of God here on Earth. We don't make the rules; we enforce The Kingdom decrees that our God established. We're called to live out God's word in such a way that our lives can eternally impact others. Our words should be seasoned with salt and grace so we can draw unbelievers to Christ. The culture of the Kingdom we represent encourages us to live in harmony with the people of our host land and to seek peace, as far as it depends on us (Romans 12:18). We are also to aim to live a life that is above reproach because our lifestyle is our witness to a dying world.

As sons and daughters of the Kingdom of God, we have a belief system and language that is strange to people of the world. The Word of God is the foundation of what we believe and serves as our constitution and guide for our life's decisions. As believers in Christ, we live with the awareness that we are foreigners and strangers on the earth. Once our ambassadorial assignment is completed, we will return to our heavenly country to serve our King for all eternity.

As Kingdom citizens, we have a distinctive language that identifies us to the Kingdom of our origin. We speak faith - a language only known by those whose heart is to please God. Our language allows us the opportunity to effectively communicate with our Heavenly Father and execute the plan He already authorized. By faith, we declare the promises of God in our lives and take the necessary actions to see them come to fruition. In the Kingdom of God, Faith is our superpower. It's the language of the empowered believer.

Since The Kingdom of God is within us, we have a responsibility to release its atmosphere and culture into our host land. There is no violence in the Kingdom of God, no sickness, no poverty, no lack, no social inequality, no corruption.

If we're going to discuss spiritual warfare, we need to focus on the fact that there are two kingdoms at war against each other. The Bible tells us in Ephesians 6:12, *"that we wrestle not against flesh and blood, but against principalities and powers, against the rulers of the darkness of this world, against spiritual wickedness in high places...*

We engage in warfare from a place of victory. We war from the finished work of the cross. We're here to reinforce what Christ has already accomplished. We're like the police enforcing the laws of the Kingdom. Just like the police system in the natural world is responsible to enforce the laws, our posture in spiritual warfare is the same. We've been given the authority to enforce the decrees of the Kingdom of God.

The Reason For Warfare

We need to understand that the two Kingdoms are at war against each other for the purpose of enforcing their dominion here on Earth. In other words, the question is, whose agenda will prevail in your life? What Kingdoms will rule our communities, our schools, and our workplaces? The spiritual fight that we're in is about the souls of men and the culture that will ultimately reign on the Earth. I believe that as Christians, we are part of the army of God, empowered to fight spiritually for the souls of men and to gain influence in every aspect of society. As believers, we have a mandate to proactively affect the culture for the glory of God. We cannot afford to be silent on matters that are important to God. We have a responsibility to be the salt and light of the earth. Your entire existence should disrupt the kingdom of darkness. The scripture clearly tells us that Jesus came to destroy the works of the devil.

As sons and daughters of God, we're called to disrupt the works of Satan and enforce the culture of the Kingdom of God.

Protect Your Faith And Your Mind

The enemy wants to discredit the character of God, and he also wants to discredit the validity of the Word of God. The devil wants to distort the perception that you have of God by sowing seeds of doubt in your mind. I've come to understand that the enemy will attack your faith, as it is the bedrock of your belief system. If he can get you to doubt every word that God has spoken about you, he can derail your path and ultimately sabotage the purposes that God has for you.

Bold As A Lion

One of the benefits of our birthright as spiritual sons and daughters of the Most High is the delegated authority we've been given in Christ. Let's be clear that as believers, the spiritual warfare in our lives is about what we carry. The enemy is intimidated by the weight of the assignment God gave you. A son and daughter of God, who understands his or her authority in Christ, is a direct target of demonic plots and deceptions. Satan, through his deceptive trickery, wants us to believe that we're helpless or incapable to overcome his attacks.

The conversations that Heaven is having about you carry more weight than the lies the enemy whispers to your ears. Regardless of how you feel about yourself, know that God is bragging about you. We have a responsibility to carry ourselves the way God sees us.

We serve The Lord of Host, The God of the Angelic Armies, who has already deployed His army to fight on our behalf. The battle is already won; the victory is already yours through Christ Jesus. No matter what your situation looks like right now, the devil cannot abort God's plans. He will try to delay it, but delay is never denial.

Just like these strong women in Hidden Figures, we each have a purpose to carry out God's plan. These women were secure in their identity, were bold in their pursuit, and had a clear sense of their callings. It's imperative to understand that God paid the highest bride price so we can recognize our birthright and walk in the fullness of our inheritance as sons and daughters of God.

Growing In Your Identity As A Son And Daughter Of God

There are elements of our Christian walk that are essential to our maturity as sons and daughters of God. Growing in our identity in Christ will require a greater level of intentionality on our part. I believe that we have a role to play as we mature in our understanding of who we are in Christ. Growing in our identity in Christ is dependent on our revelation of the concepts mentioned below.

Surrender – If you haven't given your life to Christ, I would like to invite you to do so. It's the best decision you'll ever make. If you've known Christ, but you sense that you've drifted away, you can rededicate your life to the Lord Jesus Christ.

The Word of God – Become a student of the Word of God and enroll in the school of the Holy Spirit. What I mean by that is, it's important for us to invest quality time in the Word of God, so we can renew our minds and grow in our identity in Christ. It's the knowledge that we apply that will transform our lives. If you are dealing with negative thoughts or sexual thoughts – meditate on the word of God and apply it. Set aside at least 30 mins per day to read the Word.

Prayer & Worship – Invest in spending time praying and talking to God. Prayer is a two-way communication between you and God. When you invest time in prayer, you will cultivate a deeper relationship with God, understand the mind of Christ, and blossom in His will. It has to become a lifestyle, not an event.

Faith – As mentioned earlier in the Chapter, it's impossible to please God without Faith (See Hebrews 11:6). Faith is that unwavering confidence that God will do the right thing, at the right time, in the right way according to His agenda. It's the conduit by which we receive God's promises into our lives. The good news is that our Faith has tremendous potential to grow. It can start as the smallest seed, but through spending time in the Word of God it grows significantly. Always make sure that your confessions align with the will of God regardless of what your circumstances look like. The Bible tells us that life and death is in the power of the tongue, so use your words to agree with God's plans concerning you.

Obedience – Decide in your heart that you will live a life of obedience regardless of what God asked of you. This needs to be non-negotiable. In the things of God, your obedience to His voice is the catalyst to your spiritual maturity. As sons and daughters of God, we shouldn't expect a trophy every time we obey the Lord. Obedience is a basic requirement of our sonship. It's birthed from a place of deep love and desire to please our Heavenly Father. Our continuous "yes" paves the way for our maturity.

We will further explore the idea of living a life of obedience towards the end of this chapter.

Gifts – All of us have been given multiple gifts; some are in operation, yet others are dormant. We need to activate those gifts and invest in them, so we can grow in them for the benefit of others. What I mean by investing in your gift, for instance, is if you have a gift of writing – take writing courses, so you can develop that gift. When we don't use our gifts, we are robbing society of God's blessings. The purpose of the gifts that we have in us is to be a blessing to others, to facilitate their breakthroughs, and to propel them into their destinies.

Courage – Decide that you will not allow fear to stop you from walking in the fullness of your calling as a son or daughter of God. Find courage to confront and challenge your fears. Courage is not the absence of fear, but rather, it's the willingness to confront fear head on. Even though fear will always raise its ugly head, when we decide to step out and do anything great, we have to be confident knowing that we are children of God. God didn't give us a spirit of fear. He gave us a spirit of power, love, and a sound mind.

Accountability – It's important to ask for help on our journey to growing as a son or daughter of God. Make yourself accountable to people who will hold you at the standard that the Word teaches. Look for those mentors you can receive correction, adjustment, and encouragement from. People who walk in integrity, fear, and wisdom of God and those who are committed to pouring into your life. To identify good mentors, learn by the Holy Spirit to discern who they are by their fruits and character. Surround yourself with friends and mentors, who will challenge your complacency and call out your great destiny. Stop entertaining unfruitful relationships. Invest in people of substance, who are not threatened or intimidated by the magnitude of your dreams.

Sonship/Daughtership Mindset

As a son and daughter of God who no longer identifies with the world, let me remind you to fully embrace your position in Christ. Because we've been reconciled to the Father through the sacrifice of Jesus, we've been forgiven, redeemed, and adopted as God's children. The beauty of our spiritual adoption is that God deliberately chose us. God didn't just choose us, but He also predestined each one of us to a life of purpose and significance in Christ. In God's heart and plan, He desires no one to perish. No one should live a life outside of God's will when God preordained a life of abundance in Him.

> Ephesians 1:11 declares that in Christ, *"we also were made [God's] heritage (portion) and we obtained an inheritance; for we had been foreordained (chosen and appointed beforehand) in accordance with His purpose, Who works out everything in agreement with the counsel and design of His [own] will..."* (AMPC)

Furthermore, the Bible tells us in Romans 8:15-17:

"For you have not received a spirit of slavery leading again to fear [of God's judgment], but you have received the Spirit of adoption as sons [the Spirit producing sonship] by which we [joyfully] cry, "Abba! Father!" The Spirit Himself testifies and confirms together with our spirit [assuring us] that we [believers] are children of God. And if [we are His] children, [then we are His] heirs also: heirs of God and fellow heirs with Christ [sharing His spiritual blessing and inheritance], if indeed we share in His suffering so that we may also share in His glory." Romans 8:15-17

Sonship/Daughtership is the process of maturing in intimacy with the Triune God—Father, Son, and Holy Spirit—and growing daily in a healthier understanding of Scriptures. Charles Spurgeon once said that, *"being a Christian is more than just an instantaneous conversion - it's a daily process whereby you grow to be more and more like Christ."* Christ's life represents the ultimate example of true sonship. He was one with the Father, in spirit, character, nature, and actions. We can also grow in our sonship as we imitate Christ in our daily living.

To help us better understand the progression that takes place on our continuous journey of growing as sons and daughters of God, let's look at this diagram that I put together.

Living a Lifestyle of Obedience

Obedience is the basic requirement of true sons and daughters, walking with their Father. Our obedience to the Father directly flows from our love reservoir.

> John 14:15 "If you love me, you will keep my commands."

The truth is that our proximity to our Heavenly Father is determined by our obedience. Love and obedience are interconnected in the Kingdom of God. They always walk hand in hand. The more we grow in our love and pursuit of God, the more we desire to do His will. It's all connected. Sometimes in our human thinking, what motivates us to be obedient to God's word and voice are the blessings that we believe will follow our obedience. I don't believe that our focus in pleasing our Heavenly Father should be focused on seeking a reward for our obedience. I believe the greatest rewards we could pursue in being obedient to the Father, is greater intimacy with Him. When your obedience to the Father is born from a place of love and not obligation, our reward is more of Him.

A son or daughter of God delights in pleasing their Heavenly Father regardless of whether they feel like it or not. A lover of Jesus seeks to be about the Father's business at all times. Living a life of obedience is a privilege. It reveals the depth of our love and trust for God.

What's the evidence of a mature son and daughter of God? [I'm glad you asked].

Maturity for a believer is revealed through our obedience and our representation of God's Kingdom. A believer who is sold out to Christ knows that it's an honor to partner with God to advance His Kingdom. We get to be contributors to God's divine strategies in pushing His agenda forward. A son and daughter of God who live a lifestyle of obedience have resolved in their hearts that there's nothing attractive to them outside of the will of God.

There's a level of trust that sons and daughters operate in that demonstrates complete trust in our Heavenly Father. The reality is that God's intentions towards us are always pure and right. He will never set us up to fail nor does He ask us to do something that doesn't produce good fruits. No doubt that not everything that God asked of us feels good, definitely not. However the more we walk with God, the more we grow in trusting in His divine nature. God is good and He can really be trusted.

Trusting God requires us to let go of our obsession to control things. Saying yes to God can be frightening because it often means choosing to surrender and relinquishing control. It also means coming to terms with the unknowns waiting on the other side of our obedience.

Our obedience to God's word is a direct indication of our spiritual maturity. The more you obey God and His Word, the more we grow spiritually. The more we obey God and do what He asks us to do, the more we develop a greater connection with Him.

Have you ever been disobedient? I know we all have disobeyed God's word and if you are honest, you know that it's a horrible feeling. As a mature son or daughter of God, you know that there is a consequence for our disobedience. His word clearly tells us that God corrects whom He loves. We can come to God and repent, which is good because we need to repent, but it doesn't mean we will not suffer the consequences of our actions.

In reality, our obedience is a demonstration of the love that we have for our Heavenly Father. If we love Him, we will be eager to follow His lead.

Sometimes we want God to talk to us but we get upset because God is quiet. Sometimes, God is quiet because you didn't do the last thing He told you to do. God will only repeat Himself so many times, right? At some point, He is going to stop talking till you go back and do the last thing He asked you to do. Plain and simple.

We often don't realize that our disobedience is wrapped up in our tendency to procrastinate. When we postpone doing what the Lord is asking us to do, we are delaying the fulfillment of His plans. We are also jeopardizing the many ways our stories can positively influence others. There's a reason why the Lord encourages us to act promptly when he gives us assignments because destinies are connected to our obedience.

We don't always see the bigger picture and we may not know or understand why God is telling us to do certain things but we have to trust His word, His voice, and the Holy Spirit inside of us.

The Call Of Obedience

Another story in the Bible I love is the story of Queen Esther. God specifically called Esther out of her comfort zone so she can deliver her people, the Jews. So for an entire year, she was set apart in preparation to become Queen. She was bathed in expensive perfumes and oils. She had to learn the mindset of a Queen. She was preparing herself for her night encounter with the King.

What about us, are we allowing God to set us apart so we can encounter the King of Kings? The same way Esther was purged with oils and expensive perfumes, I don't know about you but I want to be washed in God's anointing and bathed in the oil of His presence. Are we allowing the Word of God to purge our minds and adjust our attitudes so we can become vessels of honor, fit for the King to use us?

If we don't allow God to set us apart and if we are not obedient to His call, he will raise another. In the story of Esther, Her uncle Mordecai reminded her that she was born for such a time as this but that God would raise another If she was disobedient.

> *"Mordecai sent this reply to Esther: "Don't think for a moment that because you're in the palace you will escape when all other Jews are killed. If you keep quiet at a time like this, deliverance and relief for the Jews will arise from some other place, but you and your relatives will die. Who knows if perhaps you were made queen for just such a time as this?" Esther 4:13-14*

There are so many people's lives that are dependent on your obedience to God. Your decision to say "yes" to God is the key that will set captives free. People's lives are at stake, and there is an urgency to do the will of God. I encourage you to act promptly when you hear the voice of God tugging at your heart. Whether God is asking you to call a friend or start volunteering at your local homeless shelter, respond promptly when He speaks to you.

Another powerful demonstration of the call of obedience is seen in the life of our Savior Jesus Christ. The Word of God in Hebrews Chapter 5 talks about Jesus being our High Priest, but there is a verse that really reveals His humanity.

> *"In the days of His flesh [Jesus] offered up definite, special petitions [for that which He not only wanted but needed] and supplications with strong crying and tears to Him Who was [always] able to save Him [out] from*

death, and He was heard because of His reverence toward God [His godly fear, His piety, in that He shrank from the horrors of separation from the bright presence of the Father]. Although He was a Son, He learned [active, special] obedience through what He suffered And, [His completed experience] making Him perfectly [equipped], He became the Author and Source of eternal salvation to all those who give heed and obey Him,

Being designated and recognized and saluted by God as High Priest after the order (with the rank) of Melchizedek." Hebrews 5:7-10 (AMPC)

These verses reveal that Jesus, being the Son of God, still had to submit His will to God's will. If you remember in the garden of Gethsemane, before the crucifixion, Jesus said, if it was His will, He would like the cup to pass from Him but He said *"nevertheless not my will, but God's will be done."* I love that the Bible reminds us that we need to crucify our flesh daily, pick up our own cross and follow Christ. May we all learn to live a life of surrender.

The Benefits Of Walking In Obedience To God's Word:

1. When you are walking in obedience to God, He shows His faithfulness and He gives you the grace you need to be able to perform the task that He requires of you. When God tells you to do something He has already given you the ability to get it done. The key is to lean on His grace (unmerited favor) and to trust in the leading of the Holy Spirit.

"Know therefore that the Lord your God is God; he is the faithful God, keeping His covenant of love to a thousand generations of those who love him and keep His commandments." Deuteronomy 7:9 (NIV)

2. Walking in obedience to God's word unlocks prosperity.

"If they obey and serve Him, they will spend the rest of their days in prosperity and their years in contentment." Job 36:11 (NIV)

3. By walking in obedience to God's word, we become His treasure. Our lives begin to exhibit tangible evidence that we belong to Him.

"Now if you will obey me and keep my covenant, you will be my own special treasure from *among all the peoples on earth; for all the earth belongs to me." Exodus 19:5 (NIV)*

4. By walking in obedience to God's word, we have His protection.

"But if you carefully obey his voice and do all that I say, then I will be an enemy to your enemies and an adversary to your adversaries." Exodus 23:22 (NIV)

5. By walking in obedience to God's word, there is total freedom that you partake off. Because you know that the **outcome of your obedience belongs to God**, you can rest in Him and be free because you know that you completely obeyed Him. I believe that we're only responsible to obey God, the outcome and results of our obedience are completely up to God.

Where Does Our Obsession To Control The Outcomes Come From?

I believe that control issues typically stem from a deep lack of trust. People who struggle with control tendencies often like to have several contingency plans in place because of the fear of being at the mercy of others. Let's be honest, we often feel helpless when a situation is completely at the mercy of God. As much as we say that we trust God, and knowing that there are some circumstances that only He can change, it makes us very uneasy and it reveals our limitations. Additionally, a trust issue is closely associated with a lack of dependency in our relationships, but also in our interactions with God. Sometimes, people will trust God to a certain degree and at the same time arrange plans B, C, D, and E in case God's plans don't come to fruition. Believers who operate in that mindset, constantly struggle with the idea of totally surrendering to God's will. There's inevitably a constant tug of war in their hearts between fully yielding to the will of God and trusting in their own abilities.

Our inability to fully surrender to God's will, also reveals the pride in our hearts. We go about our days thinking that we're in control of our lives and that we've got everything figured out. The truth is, we deceive ourselves if we think we can control every aspect of our lives. God is the Master Planner. We've got to decide to let go of our tendency to control our lives and invite His presence into every area of our existence.

It's also interesting to me how we don't mind God using us when His request fits the boundaries of our comfort zones. But the moment what He requires of us is no longer convenient or pleasant, we start looking for ways to escape and run.

Frankly, these past few years have given me many reasons to run away from yielding to God. Isn't it easier to run and do our own thing instead of saying yes to God and choosing to embark on the journey He has for us? Maybe God has been asking you to forgive someone who hurt you, but it's a lot easier to ignore the nudges of the Holy Spirit and to pretend you didn't hear His direction, right?

How many of us have thrown tantrums because we expected life to unfold a certain way... but it didn't? Instead, life decided to throw curve balls and detours you were never prepared for. Maybe it's time to stop running and fully surrender your plans, disappointments, and pain to Jesus. There may be some areas of your life where you haven't invited Him into yet. Are you willing to say YES regardless of what the future may hold?

Will you still say yes and surrender to God's plans even through the pain? Will you still choose to love Jesus even when things don't make sense, or even when there's no guarantee that things will turn in your favor?

Our willingness to relinquish control of our lives and obey God directly stems from the love we have towards Him. The deeper your love and affection towards Christ, the more you will be willing to lay your life down for His glory. No matter the cost you have to pay.

I'm reminded in this season of my life that I can't write the script of the ways God receives the glory. In other words, if my life belongs to God, I've given Him full permission to orchestrate the details of my life. God is the author of the story of my life. He alone determines how the chapters of my life are written and the redemptive story lines that are setups to give Him the glory.

The Evidence Of Sonship/Daughtership

The blessings that God chooses to release in your life are not evidence of sonship. Just because God hasn't blessed you with the material blessings that you desire doesn't mean He's withholding sonship or daughtership from you.

What's the evidence of your sonship/daughtership? What clearly demonstrates that someone is a son or daughter of God? It's your total dependency, surrender, and willingness to emulate Christ - when the world can clearly see that His language becomes your language and when obedience is no longer a behavior you adopt to gain something, but you understand that obedience is part of who you are. I've come to realize that the reward of sonship/daughtership is greater intimacy with the Lord. A deeper walk with the Lord doesn't guarantee a release of material blessings. **Entitlement creeps in our hearts when there's an expectation that we should be rewarded with blessings for living a life of obedience.**

God Qualifies His Son & Daughter

We've all felt inadequate at some point on our journey. You know that feeling you get when you don't think you qualify for something, or you just don't think that God can use your life in a great way. The fact remains that God doesn't call the qualified; instead, He qualifies the called.

I can't even count the number of times I've felt inadequate or not qualified enough. Whether it was for a job opportunity that was offered to me or a speaking opportunity, I've always felt like David, when Samuel was looking to anoint the next King (1 Samuel 16). When Samuel went to Jesse's house, David wasn't even lined up as his seven brothers stood before Samuel to be selected. David was outside, tending sheep and minding his own business.

Can you believe that David's family didn't even consider him as a candidate to the throne? That's awful. This tells me that sometimes, your own family will not see the God-given potential lying dormant inside of you. A future King was in their house and they didn't even recognize it. All they saw was David's inadequacies and shortcomings. Meanwhile, God saw David's great potential.

> "But the Lord said to Samuel, "Do not look at his appearance or at his physical stature, because I have refused him. For the Lord does not see as man sees; for man looks at the outward appearance, but the Lord looks at the heart." 1 Samuel 16:7 (NKJV)

While Samuel was about to select one of David's brothers, God revealed to him that the heart of men is really what He is after. It's interesting how people can disqualify you because you may not fit their standard of beauty or because they think you look a little awkward. Sometimes, people won't necessarily champion you because you're a quiet leader and not necessarily charismatic.

I believe that you have the capacity to become everything that our Heavenly Father says about you. Christ in you is the seed that will develop into the character of God. That's the essence of sonship and daughtership. What the Lord has spoken over your life will come to fruition as you continue to partner with Him. What He sees you becoming is a reflection of God's very nature. You're good enough, smart enough, and capable enough for everything the Lord has called you to accomplish.

As I'm writing this chapter of the book, I'm also sensing in my heart that someone needs to be reminded not to despise the days of humble beginnings. Your humble beginnings represent a training ground for the next level God is calling you to. God is using your current situation to mold and shape your character, because where you are heading, your character needs to be solid enough to sustain you.

You may be doing a job, like David, that is below your potential, but God is saying that if you remain faithful, He will elevate you. Continue to look to Him and not to men. God is the source of your promotion. As a son and daughter of God, we've got to trust in His ability to orchestrate the details of our lives. Jeremiah 29:11 tells us that God's plans are to prosper us and not to harm us. Plans to give us a future and a hope (my paraphrase). The question is, *"do we fully trust God with the details of our lives?"* If we're honest with ourselves, at times we feel as if we know what's best for us. Our actions sometimes reveal our inability to give God full control of the steering wheel of our life. It's interesting that oftentimes, God promotes those that the world perceives as being "least likely to succeed." I love the way God uses foolish things to confound the wise. Who can comprehend the ways of God? God is so amazing! I love it when He transforms someone's life for His glory.

That's why we should never give up on people, because God is the one who chooses and qualifies. You may know someone, who seems to have all odds stacked up against them, and things don't seem to look too good for that person. I'm persuaded that God is permanently attracted to the rejected and the outcasts. What people often forget is that God can take a homeless man and turn him into a businessman. God can do anything. When it comes to God's amazing plan for His children, your past doesn't determine your future. When you have a personal relationship with Jesus Christ, His blood covers your sins and your past is forgotten.

Our focus should never be on the things that can potentially disqualify us. Some people will think that you are too young to lead them or too young to start a business. Others will want to disqualify you because you are a woman. Some will say that you are too old, or you are not charismatic enough, or you don't have enough experience. Others will say that the competition is fierce, and you don't have the credentials and the degrees to stay in the race.

But God! When God calls you, He doesn't need men's approval or validation. **When the world looks at your resume, God looks at your potential, because He sees what you are becoming in Him.**

Do you know the story of Gideon from Judges 6? Gideon was a young man, from a poor family, collecting wheat when the Angel of the Lord appeared to him. God told Gideon that he was to lead the Nation of Israel into battle and to overthrow the altar of Baal, who was a false god. Sometimes we may find what God wants us to do impossible because we focus on our personality, inadequacy, or our lack of resources.

God called Gideon a mighty man of valor even when Gideon didn't see himself in that light. It's powerful to me that God always addresses you as the person you already are in the Spirit realm. God already saw the triumphant victories Gideon was going to win as the leader of Israel. And as the story unfolds, we see that God used Gideon in a mighty way to defeat the Midianites. Gideon went from being a farmer to being the fifth judge of the Nation of Israel.

Did you ever notice that God never calls people by their past? It's the devil who always calls us by our weaknesses, our sins, or by our past. People will also label you by your past, but our Heavenly Father always speaks to our potential in Him. God is always interested in who you are becoming and not who you were.

That's why the words you speak over your life matter. Your future is dependent on the words you agree with today. What are you prophesying over your present and future? What do you call yourself? Align yourself with who God sees in you, and stop entertaining the lies of the enemies.

> *"Death and life are in the power of the tongue, and they who indulge in it shall eat the fruit of it [for death or life]." Proverbs 18:21* (AMPC)

What are you declaring out of your mouth? Who are you agreeing with? Speak only those things that are in alignment with the word that your Heavenly Father has declared over you.

You can sabotage your life if you come into agreement with negative words or destructive thoughts. It's important to watch your mouth and the words you speak over yourself. Don't sabotage what God is preparing for you by speaking words like "I can't" or "I will never be able to..."

When the world defines you by your flaws or emphasizes your inadequacies, God calls you by His name. He poured out His Spirit in you when you committed your life to Christ (If you haven't done so, invite Jesus into your heart and ask Him to be your Lord and Savior—also read Romans 10:9).

So, any time I feel inadequate, I remind myself that God is the One who called me. I didn't call myself. He is the One who appointed and qualified me for the assignment He has prepared for me. I am good enough because of the sacrifice Jesus Christ made on Calvary for my sins and my freedom. When He said, *"it is finished,"* He nailed my sins, my shame, and my insecurities to the cross. The world can no longer label me; my past has no power over me.

God wants to use you and all you have to do is yield. Say YES to Jesus, daily!

Affirmations of Sons and Daughters of God

Because you are in Christ, every single one of these statements directly applies to you.

Declare these affirmations out loud as often as you're led to. There's tremendous power in speaking the truth of God's Word over your life.

- I am loved (1 John 3:3).
- I am accepted (Ephesians 1:6).
- I am a son/daughter of God (John 1:12).
- I am united with God and one Spirit with Him (1 Corinthians 6:17).
- I am a joint heir with Jesus, sharing His inheritance with Him (Romans 8:17).
- I am the temple of the Holy Spirit (1 Corinthians 6:19).
- I am redeemed and forgiven (Colossians 1:14).
- I am fully complete in Christ (Colossians 2:10).

- I am free from condemnation (Romans 8:1).
- I am a new creation in Christ (2 Corinthians 5:17).
- I am established and anointed by God (2 Corinthians 1:21).
- I do not operate in fear (2 Timothy 1:7).
- I am seated in Heavenly places with Christ (Ephesians 2:6).
- I have direct access to God (Ephesians 2:18).
- I walk with God daily because He never leaves me (Hebrews 13:5).

Prophetic Declaration

Trust Without Borders

The Lord loves you! Never give up on His promises. Ask God to lead you every step of the way. He will never leave you, nor forsake you. Trust and believe that the best is yet to come, even when you don't understand the details of your life. Do not forget that God is still on the throne. Do not be discouraged, child of God; there's purpose in the process. God said that He will be with you. If God is for you, who can be against you? Be strong and courageous, for the Lord is with you wherever you go. Trust and believe. Know that God has a big plan for you. The plan that He has for you will not be aborted. Hold on to every single promise and realize that God is your Father.

I hear the Lord say:

> *"I'm taking you into greater realms of trust, where you will understand that no man can orchestrate the details of your life. You belong to me alone. I have you right in the palms of my hands, and I know what is best for you. Do not be discouraged, and do not be fearful. Even through the fire, I'm with you. I will perform every single word according to my divine timing. Be patient and realize that the best is still ahead of you. Your efforts are not in vain, but you need to understand that without me,*

you can do nothing. I make things grow; I provide the increase and the miracle. Everything you need is in me, not in your own abilities. I love you, and I will carry you through the seasons of life.

Believe in my promises. Put your trust in my words and you will not be disappointed. I'm healing your expectations and aligning you with my divine order. The time is now for me to execute the great plan that I have for you. I had to break you, so that when it happens, your flesh would not interfere with all I have ordained in your life. You haven't tasted yet the fullness of my goodness. Get ready! Get ready! Your best days are still ahead of you!

Taste and see that I'm good. I'm good to you, my child. Open your heart, be ready to be blown away. Lift up your eyes and witness the glory of God over your life. Trust me, even when you don't understand. I'm taking you into realms you've never been. The journey will be worth it."

6

Created for Intimacy

In this chapter, we are going to look at how to develop a deeper relationship with the Holy Spirit and the benefits of cultivating a deeper friendship with Him.

Sometimes I hear believers identify the Holy Spirit as "something" or an "it" because of a lack of understanding of who the Holy Spirit actually is. Some Christians have a habit of saying that "something" told them to go to the store, or "something" told them to check on their children or to call their friend. I'm here to remind us that the Holy Spirit is not an "it." The Holy Spirit is a Person of the Trinity. He is the Spirit of the living God dwelling inside of us the moment we make a heart commitment to surrender our lives to the leadership of Christ. The same Spirit of God, who created the Earth, and who was hovering over the surface of the waters, resides inside of us. The same Spirit and the same power that raised Christ from the dead lives in us.

As believers, we know that we serve one God: God the Father, God the Son, and God the Holy Spirit, who equals One God. The Bible tells us in Romans 3:23 that we've all sinned and fallen short of the glory of God. That's why, from the beginning, our sins separated us from God. But because of God's amazing love towards us, He provided a way for us to be reconciled with Him. That's when God made Himself flesh and came on Earth as our Lord Jesus Christ, so He can reconcile us to Himself the moment we confess our sins and accept Him into our hearts. Then the Holy Spirit comes inside of us, partners with our human spirit, and empowers us to live the Christian walk.

The Scriptures tell us that God not only has established every believer in Christ, but He has also anointed us and has sealed us by giving us His Holy Spirit as a guarantee of our salvation (2 Corinthians 1:21-22). In other words, The Holy Spirit is the deposit or down payment that the Lord has invested in us towards the full manifestation of the promise of eternal life awaiting us. The workings of the Holy Spirit in our lives is proof of our spiritual adoption as God's children. There's tremendous value for every born again believer to intentionally grow in our understanding of the Holy Spirit and to develop deeper intimacy with Him.

According to the Merriam-Webster dictionary, the word "intimacy" is defined as a quality that suggests closeness, a sense of belonging, and the idea of inseparability in relationships. When you're intimate with people, there's often a comfort in knowing them personally and being familiar with the core of their personhood. Intimacy in friendship doesn't happen overnight. It's a process of investing quality time in nurturing a strong rapport and bond with the person.

True intimacy requires vulnerability, a growing trust factor, and the willingness to let go of our self-sufficient mindset. Often, in relationships, people never experience the beauty of a mature friendship because of all the impenetrable walls they have erected around their hearts. Many people approach their relationship with the Holy Spirit in the same way. We can't enjoy the fruit of a deep connection with Him if we don't allow Him access to every part of our heart. Developing a relationship with the Spirit of the Living God requires us to embrace an ongoing posture of surrender. We need to make a commitment to let go of our need for self-preservation and our obsession for independence and control.

It's the Father's desire, through His Holy Spirit, to establish an interdependence culture in our relationship with Him. When we develop an interdependence mindset, there's a mutual reliance that exists between the parties. We then begin to cooperate more effectively with the Holy Spirit to accomplish the will of Father-God. The Holy Spirit needs our "yes" to work in and through us to further advance the Kingdom of God.

In getting to know The Holy Spirit on a deeper level over the years, I realized that He is not just an expert in spiritual matters. As the Spirit of God, He is all-knowing and a great source of revelation and divine wisdom in every field of life. If you seek Him, He will give you divine strategies and direction for your business, solutions in your boardroom, wisdom for your marriage, and a blueprint to raise world changers. When we rely too much on our human intellect and physical senses, it hinders us from fully trusting the Spirit of the living God. **We've got to deepen our intimacy with the Holy Spirit to heighten the accuracy of our spiritual radar.** As we intentionally seek to grow in our pursuit of God's Holy Spirit, we will become more and more Spirit-led and less circumstance-driven.

Let's look at Jesus' encouragement to the disciples in John 16:7-13, so we can dive deeper into the character and nature of God-The Holy Spirit.

> *"Nevertheless I tell you the truth. It is to your advantage that I go away; for if I do not go away, **The Helper** will not come to you; but if I depart, I will send Him to you. And when He has come, He will convict the world of sin, and of righteousness, and of judgment: of sin, because they do not believe in Me; of righteousness, because I go to My Father and you see Me no more; of judgment, because the ruler of this world is judged.*
>
> *"I still have many things to say to you, but you cannot bear them now. However, when He, **The Spirit of truth**, has come, He will **guide you into all truth;** for He will not speak on His own authority, but whatever He hears He will speak; and He will tell you things to come." John 16:7-13 (NKJV)*

When we look at this passage of Scripture, Jesus was preparing the disciples, because He was soon going to depart from them, so the Holy Spirit could come. This passage describes the Holy Spirit as The Helper, The Spirit of Truth, and the One who will guide us into all truth. Other reliable translations of the Bible describe the Holy Spirit as The Comforter, The Advocate, The

Teacher, The Counselor, and Intercessor. The King James version uses the word "Comforter", which is transliterated in Greek as *paraklētos* and has several powerful meanings *(Strong's G3875-Blue Letter Bible)*. According to the Blue Letter Bible, *paraklētos* means one who pleads another's cause before a judge, a legal assistant, an advocate, an intercessor, a succourer. As Jesus stated in John 16, the role of the Holy Spirit is to journey with us in revealing deeper truths of the Gospel and giving us the strength and power we need to represent the Godhead as we continue to advance God's divine agenda.

James W. Goll, author and writer of the article titled *"Holy Spirit, You Are Welcome Here,"* gave an excellent description of the Holy Spirit's character and work:

> *"The often-quiet Holy Spirit is not a retiring Spirit—He is an activist. He is the dynamic power that Jesus promised to the Church before Pentecost. He executes the purposes and plans of the Godhead. As the One who carries out God's purposes—His creativity, inspiration, conviction, regeneration, generosity, enlightenment, sanctification, and much more—He is always working (see John 5:17).[9]*
>
> *Simply by paying attention to what He is doing and by cooperating with Him, we come to understand God better. He might be working behind the scenes and He might be bursting forth with a flame of fire, with a mighty display of power; but know this, the Holy Spirit is the Third Person of God and where He is welcomed, He has all the more liberty to do the Father's good pleasure."*

Additionally, we understand that the Holy Spirit mainly operates in two ways:

A. The Holy Spirit works within us through the process of sanctification. However, He first convicts us of ways that are contrary to God's nature. Conviction is a matter of the heart. It's the process that the Holy Spirit uses to uncover our sins and to shine the light of God's word in our hearts. The ultimate goal of the Holy Spirit working within us is to transform us into the image of Jesus Christ. In other words, the purpose of the Holy Spirit working within us is for transformation towards spiritual maturity as we continue to grow as sons and daughters of God.

B. The Holy Spirit works through us. The purpose of the Holy Spirit working through us is to reveal Jesus Christ to the world. If we go back to the Scripture in John 16:14, we understand that the purpose of the Holy Spirit working through us is to glorify and reveal Jesus Christ to the world. Kathryn Kuhlman - one of the most influential Evangelists of our generation - often said in her messages that *"The Holy Spirit is the greatest promoter who ever lived, and He promotes just one person: Jesus Christ."* John 15:26-27 records Jesus declaring to His disciples that the Comforter whom the Father will send, will testify of Him.

Our responsibility is to allow the Holy Spirit to work within us and through us. We have to be careful because sometimes we can be an interference to the work of the Holy Spirit. Our stubborn nature can often delay God's work from coming to fruition. The Holy Spirit is a gentleman, He will not force Himself on anybody. We have to be willing to change when the Holy Spirit convicts our hearts. We have to be prompt enough to be obedient on the spot and not delay His plans. We have to humble ourselves and allow Him to mold us. It's a refining process, and sometimes it's painful, but the Holy Spirit has to remove everything that displeases Him so our lives continue to reflect the life of Jesus.

Some years ago, there was a particular season of my life when my mother and I were struggling to get along. We would always get into major disagreements almost every week. It was an emotionally and mentally exhausting time of my life. My attitude was constantly defensive towards her. It was a very frustrating season as we weren't seeing eye to eye on a lot of important matters. Our relationship at the time was not enjoyable, and it was clearly bothering me. So I started seeking the Holy Spirit on a deeper level, asking Him to help me establish a better rapport with my mother.

At the time, I would ask the Holy Spirit to convict my mother of her shortcomings, so she can change her ways. Can you believe that?! I didn't think that I was doing or saying anything wrong. (Good Lord Almighty, Thank God for maturity!) However, the more I was focusing on the things that my mother was doing that were upsetting me, the more the Holy Spirit was narrowing His focus on my character and the many ways that I needed to change.

Little did I know that the Holy Spirit was about to thrust me into a whole transformation journey. The Holy Spirit confronted the pride of my heart and gently showed me the errors of my ways. He then revealed to me that I wasn't very teachable in that season, nor was I remotely willing to learn from my mother. Ouch! It stinks when the Holy Spirit convicts you. Those *"coming to Jesus moments"* don't feel too good, but they are defining moments that liberate us. The truth shall indeed set us free, if we receive.

When I humbled myself and gave the Holy Spirit room to work on me, my focus was no longer on my mother's behavior. It's been over a decade of continually giving permission to the Holy Spirit to perfect His work in me. Because I stopped fighting God's transformation process, I became pliable in His hands. As a result of yielding to God's process, I've seen the Lord beautify my relationship with my mother. Our conversations and interactions over the years have become a lot more life-giving. The quality of our relationship has drastically shifted from what it used to be. What a faithful God we serve! He is still in the business of changing lives, and oftentimes, it starts with the person in the mirror.

Let's look at the Scriptures in 2 Timothy 2:20-21:

> *"But in a great house there are not only vessels of gold and silver, but also [utensils] of wood and earthenware, and some for honorable and noble [use] and some for menial and ignoble [use].*
>
> *So whoever cleanses himself [from what is ignoble and unclean, **who separates himself from contact with contaminating and corrupting influences]** will [then himself] **be a vessel set apart and useful for honorable and noble purposes, consecrated and profitable to the***

Master, fit and ready for any good work." (AMPC)

Hallelujah! If we allow the Holy Spirit to mold us and refine us, He will use us for great work. So many people want to be used by God, but don't want to go through the pruning and refining process. The only validation of our very existence as followers of Jesus Christ is the presence and ongoing work of the Holy Spirit in us. It's the power of the Holy Spirit inside of us that makes the difference.

Cultivating A Relationship With The Holy Spirit

Let's look at practical ways to grow deeper in our relationship with the Holy Spirit of God.

A.W Tozer once said, *"We can't walk with the Holy Ghost unless we agree to walk the way He walks and go in the direction He's going."* If we're going to develop a friendship with the Holy Spirit, we need to commit to a lifelong relationship process. Friendship with the Holy Spirit doesn't happen just on Sundays. You've got to be committed to getting to know Him for the long haul. If we desire a deep friendship with the Holy Spirit, it will require an investment of love, care, reciprocity, nourishment, and quality time in order to grow the relationship to a place of maturity.

I don't know about you, but I want the Holy Spirit to feel welcomed in my home. I want to make room for Him, and I want Him to know that *"mi casa es su casa."* In other words, my temple is completely His. My life is not my own. I belong to the Godhead, so everything concerning me already belongs to the Holy Spirit. In my home, The Holy Spirit is not a guest, He's a very important member of the family. He's not a visitor who needs to call before stopping by the house. The Holy Spirit is looking for a place of habitation in us; may we welcome Him in our lives with hearts wide open.

Communicate With The Holy Spirit

Develop a greater awareness of the Holy Spirit as you deliberately think about Him as you go about your day. Talk to Him throughout the day and journal the thoughts He highlights in your spirit. Ask Him for guidance, grace, and whatever else you need. Thank Him, praise Him, glorify Him in your heart. Think of Him before you take a step, before you open your mouth, and let Him shape your thoughts. Talk to Him during the day as you would talk to a best friend. A healthy relationship is a two-way street, It's that simple. Take time to listen to His nudges and whispers. Quiet your soul, get rid of the distractions competing for your attention. Focus your gaze on Him and you'll become a lot more sensitive to His voice and leading.

Embracing Vulnerability in Friendship

We need to be vulnerable with the Holy Spirit and uncover the things we are dealing with. Don't be embarrassed to share how you truly feel about what you're going through. We need to grow in our ability to trust the Holy Spirit with our pain, our joys, and our disappointments - that's the only way we can be healed. The Spirit of the Living God already knows all your thoughts and frustrations, so there's nothing hidden from His sight. When we verbalize what we're going through and share those experiences with The Holy Spirit, we give Him space to hear His heart on those matters.

Quality Time in Prayer

When you love someone, you want to spend quality time with that person. There is an investment of your time that is necessary in order for you to cultivate an intimate relationship with the Holy Spirit. Set a specific time for a date with the Holy Spirit on a daily basis. Remember this should not be about the length of time but the quality of the time you devote to hanging out in His presence. It could be 20 mins, 35 mins or even 45 mins a day. What matters the most is your undivided attention being turned towards intentionally growing in knowing God The Holy Spirit.

Quality Time in the Word

It's important to invest quality time in the word of God to get to know the author of the Bible. When you spend time in the word of God, you will know the mind of God. You will know the attributes of the Spirit of God. The more we invest quality time in the Word of God, the more the Word of God will shape our thinking. Make it a priority to consume the Word of God, to digest it, and apply it to your daily life. When we do so, the Holy Spirit begins to change our fleshly desires and aligns our wants to God's heart. The more you study the Word of God, the more you will grow in your knowledge and understanding of the Godhead.

The Benefits Of A Deep Relationship With The Holy Spirit

The Holy Spirit is our Teacher and Guide

He is the Spirit of Truth. He leads us into all truth and He makes us aware when we are outside of the will of God. I don't know about you but I've been disobedient a few times in my walk with The Lord and the Holy Spirit quickly convicted me and led me back to the truth. If you need wisdom and understanding, or if you are lacking clarity and specific guidance for your life, The Holy Spirit will lead you and guide you.

The Holy Spirit is Our Encourager

He gives us peace, hope, and confidence. He gives us the courage and the confidence to get up and persevere. Romans 8:26 declares:

> *"Likewise the Spirit also helps in our weaknesses. For we do not know what we should pray for as we ought, but the Spirit Himself makes intercession for us with groanings which cannot be uttered." (NKJV)*

Intimacy with the Holy Spirit Produces Power and Boldness

The power of God is available to every believer through the Holy Spirit, who dwells inside of us. Jesus tells his disciples in Acts 1:8:

"But you will receive power and ability when the Holy Spirit comes upon you; and you will be My witnesses [to tell people about Me] both in Jerusalem and in all Judea, and Samaria, and even to the ends of the earth." (AMPC)

The Holy Spirit enables us to boldly proclaim the gospel and empowers us to live it out loud. That spiritual power, strength, and divine ability is given to us, not for our own gain, but rather, to be instruments that God can use to perform miracles that will glorify The Father and advance His Kingdom.

Intimacy With The Holy Spirit Produces The Fruit Of His Character

The Holy Spirit's work in the life of the believer is marked by a commitment to sanctify and purify us into the image and likeness of our Lord Jesus Christ. We bear much fruit by walking with the Holy Spirit according to Galatians 5:22. Through the workings of the Holy Spirit within us, He has the power and ability to produce in us greater love, joy, peace, patience, kindness, goodness, self-control, faithfulness, gentleness.

Cultivating The Presence Of God

The presence of God is the manifestation of His person hood revealed in a particular atmosphere or through a willing vessel who acts as His conduit. As children of the Most High God, we're called to carry His presence everywhere we go. We're living in a time when Scriptures say in Joel 2:28 that God will pour out His Spirit on all flesh. I'm grateful that we can receive the indwelling of God's Holy Spirit the moment we become followers of Jesus. God's Spirit takes complete residence in us and partners with our human spirit.

Back in ancient days, the presence of God dwelt in the Ark of the Covenant, which was located in the Holy of Holies inside the Tabernacle Tent that God instructed Moses to build. In those days, only Priests had access to God's presence. However, this setup wasn't God's original intent for His people. God desired that the nation of Israel be a Kingdom of Priests, where He would establish a direct relationship with His people. It's always been God's intention to have intimate fellowship with us.

When we look at the Scriptures in Exodus Chapters 19 & 20, we see the Israelites experienced God's powerful presence in a tangible way at Mount Sinai. God's presence manifested as a rushing wind accompanied by smoke and fire. God's thundering voice and the manifestation of His presence terribly frightened His people to the point that they decided to appoint Moses as their spokesperson.

> *"Now all the people perceived the thunderings and the lightning and the noise of the trumpet and the smoking mountain, and as [they] looked they trembled with fear and fell back and stood far off.*
>
> *And they said to Moses, You speak to us and we will listen, but let not God speak to us, lest we die.*
>
> *And Moses said to the people, **"Fear not; for God has come to prove you, so that the [reverential] fear of Him may be before you, that you may not sin."*** Exodus* 20:18-20 (AMPC)

The same God who had delivered the Israelites from the bondage of the Egyptians is the same One who gave them the 10 Commandments and re-established His covenant with them at Mount Sinai. I've come to understand that as humans, we often misunderstand the heart of the Father towards us because of the ways He chooses to manifest His presence to us. God's reverential fear was never designed to drive us away from His presence. Revering God's presence should produce in us a holy heart posture that sets the standard by which we approach God. Because of Jesus' sacrifice through the finished work of the cross, we received the confidence to continuously draw closer to the presence of God. Hebrews 10:19-22 declares:

> *"Therefore, brethren, since we have full freedom and confidence to enter into the [Holy of] Holies [by the power and virtue] in the blood of Jesus,*
>
> *By this fresh (new) and living way which He initiated and dedicated and opened for us through the separating curtain (veil of the Holy of Holies), that is, through His flesh,*

And since we have [such] a great and wonderful and noble Priest [Who rules] over the house of God,

Let us all come forward and draw near with true (honest and sincere) hearts in unqualified assurance and absolute conviction engendered by faith (by that leaning of the entire human personality on God in absolute trust and confidence in His power, wisdom, and goodness), having our hearts sprinkled and purified from a guilty (evil) conscience and our bodies cleansed with pure water." Hebrews 10:19-22 (AMPC)

The blood of Jesus and our acceptance of His work gives us boldness to approach God's throne without trembling, fear, guilt, or shame. Through the cross, Jesus has torn down the veil that has long separated us from entering and dwelling in the Presence of God. We now have been given the opportunity to abide in God's presence and become His permanent dwelling place.

There is a dying world out there, and it's time that followers of Christ become carriers of His presence. Wherever we go, we need to carry the presence of God within us so the Holy Spirit can work through us.

What Produces Intimacy With The Holy Spirit?

- Spending time with God
- Worshipping God for who He is and not for what He can give us
- Focus on God's character and attributes but not on His gifts
- Prioritize God's desires; put Him first
- Cultivating His presence
- Embracing what pleases Him
- Identifying with His Pain
- Studying the Word of God and meditating on His Word

When I think about intimacy, the Word exclusive comes to mind. Intimacy requires sacrifice, you need to sacrifice time. Quality time is one of the most important things that we can give. Cultivating the presence of the Holy Spirit also means asking Him to increase our appetite and hunger for more of Him.

> *"[Not in your own strength] for it is **God Who is all the while effectually at work in you [energizing and creating in you the power and desire], both to will and to work for His good pleasure and satisfaction and delight.** If you find yourself in a season in which your desire to know more of God is diminished, ask The Holy Spirit to fan the fire in you again and create a greater hunger to know the Godhead better." Philippians 2:12 (AMPC)*

Intimacy is knowing God and deeply desiring to be like Him. When I think about my friendship with God - The Holy Spirit, I think about the many ways I've found fulfillment through my connection with Him. He's comforted me in ways that no human relationship could. He's been guiding me through life's detours and transitions and has enabled me to make decisions that are in alignment with The Father's will.

Let's take a moment to ponder on these questions and engage in a time of self-reflection.

> **What or who do you depend on to fill the empty places in your heart? Who or what is your source of satisfaction and fulfillment?**

These questions reminded me of one of my favorite Bible verses.

> *"Delight yourself in the Lord, And He shall give you the desires of your heart." Psalm 37:4 (NKJV)*

The Merriam-Webster dictionary defines the word "delight" as the ability to find pleasure in someone whose actions or very presence produces feelings of pleasure, gratitude, joy, and deep satisfaction.

Whether you are single or married, or in a complicated entanglement, we need to know that there is no human being who can satisfy our internal needs for love, acceptance, approval, affirmation, or comfort. Only God can speak to our desire for validation. So, one of my love languages is words of affirmation, meaning that I like for people to affirm me through words. But let me tell you that there aren't enough encouraging words that can heal my soul. Those insecurities that we hide so well, no human being can speak to those hidden places.

God knows you intimately, and He is the only One who can heal you and make you whole. The problem is that many of us don't allow God to touch those deep areas of hurt; we have to invite him into our hearts. We have to be willing to be vulnerable before God and be real. The moment we decide to allow God in our hearts, especially in those painful areas, we will experience His love.

> *"I knew you before I formed you in your mother's womb. Before you were born I set you apart and appointed you as my prophet to the nations." Jeremiah 1:5*

> *"O Lord, You search me and You know me; you know when I sit and when I stand, you understand my thoughts from afar....behind and before you encircle me and rest your hand upon me....You formed my inmost being, you knit me together in my mother's womb." Psalm 139:10-13*

The more we know God, the more we become one with Him. When we become one with Him, His desires become our desires. When you become one with God, the only thing that will satisfy your heart is pleasing Him. The closer we walk with God, the more we become holy, because God works on our hearts, and He purifies our motives.

Holiness is about imitating God's very nature, a state of total devotion to God and being set apart. God wants us to be holy as He is holy.

> *"Follow God's example, therefore, as dearly loved children and walk in the way of love, just as Christ loved us and gave himself up for us as a*

133

fragrant offering and sacrifice to God. But among you, there must not be even a hint of sexual immorality, or of any kind of impurity, or of greed, because these are improper for God's holy people." Ephesians 5:1-3

Holiness is a byproduct of intimacy with God. As we draw closer to God, He draws closer to us, we partake of His nature, and we become like Him. Holiness is a matter of the heart. As we pursue intimacy with God, we will find ourselves liking what God likes and rejecting what God doesn't like. That's what holiness and purity is about, becoming more and more like Jesus Christ. We need to know that we are not holy apart from Christ, and we cannot attain holiness through works.

"Our righteous acts are like filthy rags." Isaiah 64:6

The term *"filthy rags"* is a strong statement. So, I researched the statement and found that the word *filthy* is a translation of the Hebrew word *iddah*, which literally means the bodily fluids from a woman's menstrual cycle. The word *rags* is a translation of *begged*, meaning a rag or garment. Therefore, these "righteous acts" are considered by God as repulsive as a soiled feminine hygiene product.

This means that no one is good apart from God. Holiness is only obtained through intimacy with God; it's not about being self-righteous like I was before God opened my eyes.

What Hinders Intimacy With The Holy Spirit?

Developing a deeper intimacy with God - The Holy Spirit - also means being aware of what grieves Him. To grieve the Holy Spirit is to deeply wound Him and cause Him pain and sorrow. We can either draw the Holy Spirit or repel His presence by the way we choose to live our lives. The thoughts we meditate on, the language and words we choose to use as part of our vocabulary, and the attitude of our hearts can all play a factor in the quality of our relationship with the Holy Spirit. Below is a list of other things that can hinder our relationship with The Holy Spirit:

- Sin
- Pride
- Disobedience
- Unforgiveness in our hearts
- Know-it-all attitude (lack of teachability)
- Lack of reverence and honor for God's Word
- Entertaining distractions

I believe that God wants us to know Him intimately because He wants to transform us into the image of His son Jesus Christ. God wants us to experience His love and to know Him, not know of Him. I believe that the Spirit of God is drawing us because He wants to heal us and make us whole. God is the only one who can touch our hearts and speak to those areas of hurt, pain, and insecurities. Each one of us belongs to God. He is our Father. May we learn to seek our Heavenly Father through intimacy with His Holy Spirit. Our lives are not our own. We're God's Holy Temple; may we continue to give Him access to what already belongs to Him.

7

Becoming Whole

> *"For I will restore health to you, and I will heal your wounds, says the Lord, because they have called you an outcast, saying, This is Zion, whom no one seeks after and for whom no one cares!" Jeremiah 30:17 (AMPC)*

At six years old, she was repeatedly raped and completely robbed of her innocence and childhood. The men who were supposed to protect her, love, and care for her turned into her perpetual nightmare. For years, promiscuity and a life of debauchery became her escape and her only means of income. All she knew was exchanging her body parts for the hope to feed the child she birthed in pain. Her heart was hurting and completely broken, refusing to forgive the rapist who took her virginity.

One day, God saw her tears and said it was enough—enough of the shame, hurt, and pain-numbing the heart God created to love. Unforgiveness chained her heart and confined her to a life of bitterness until His light broke through her darkest night. As warm tears rolled down her cheeks, she clearly heard the voice of God say, *"My daughter, I will turn your pain into purpose."*

It's only the love of Christ that has the power to heal areas of deep wounds, shame, or pain that stem from our past experiences. To cope with life, some of us have medicated our pain by looking for love, significance, and acceptance in the wrong places. No human being or worldly possession was designed to bring healing to those areas of our hearts. No one can affirm you the way our Heavenly Father will. God can use your pain as a platform to your deliverance and freedom. Nothing you've endured will be wasted. Absolutely nothing. God will definitely use your anguish to birth forth His purposes.

Isaiah 62:3 declares:

> "The LORD will hold you in His hands for all to see — a splendid crown in the hands of God. Never again will you be called the Godforsaken City or the Desolate Land. Your new name will be the City of God's Delight and the Bride of God, for the LORD delights in you and will claim you as His own." (The Living Bible)

You were created in God's image, a vessel set apart to show forth God's glory. God wants to take you from pain to purpose. His desire is to equip you to forgive, teach you His ways, and propel you to fully walk in your divine purpose for the glory of His name.

The story above is inspired by a woman who shared her testimony at a Women's Conference I had the opportunity to speak at. On that day, broken and wounded women gathered for an appointment with God. For many, that day was the catalyst to their freedom and restoration. As the Holy Spirit moved on the hearts of His daughters, many were affirmed, impacted, and challenged to rise up to the great potential locked within them. We declared on that day that we will no longer be defined by our past. We believe that we are God's delight, set apart as vessels of honor, to manifest His plans on the earth. We proclaimed that from that day forward, we will be God's authentic voices and represent Him well in every arena He called us to influence.

Regardless of what you've been through, God has the capacity to restore you and make you whole.

The Process Of Wholeness

The concept of wholeness is very interesting to me. It's definitely a topic that we can unpack for days and still have enough content. The Oxford English dictionary defines wholeness as the state of being complete and forming a harmonious whole. It also mentions being unbroken or undamaged. Wholeness often indicates a good physical, mental, and overall healthy well-being. As I was pondering and meditating on the idea of growing in wholeness, I first wanted to establish a fundamental truth. As born again believers, in Christ we are complete. When we place our faith in Christ, we are united and joined to Him for eternity. Our acceptance of His sacrifice makes us whole.

In fact, Colossians 2:9-10 presents the case for our wholeness:

> "For in Him the whole fullness of Deity (the Godhead) continues to dwell in bodily form [giving complete expression of the divine nature].
> And **you are in Him, made full and having come to fullness of life [in Christ you too are filled with the Godhead—Father, Son, and Holy Spirit—and reach full spiritual stature].** And He is the Head of all rule and authority [of every angelic principality and power]." (AMPC)

The Living Bible also gives a great translation that I would like to highlight:

> "For in Christ there is all of God in a human body; **so you have everything when you have Christ, and you are filled with God through your union with Christ.** He is the highest Ruler, with authority over every other power." Colossians 2:9-10 (The Living Bible)

In Christ, our spirit is filled with the fullness of God. However, our soul (mind/intellect, will, and emotions) is being made whole as we go through the process of life. That process of growing in unity with Christ is an ongoing journey of maturation until we meet Him in eternity.

Wholeness is also the state of evolving into the likeness of Christ. It's an aspect of our spiritual wellness that involves both healing and growth. Change is inevitable, but growth is optional. When life happens, we're forced to change and adjust, but it doesn't necessarily mean that we're growing. Growth is very intentional. If we want to progressively develop into the character of Christ, we will often have to unlearn mindsets and thinking patterns that are contrary to God's character.

If we really look at the word of God, we will notice that everything about the way God does things involves a system of change, development, and growth. God's always taking us from light to darkness, from drinking milk as a newborn baby Christian to desiring the meat of the Word. We see that the Word of God is constantly provoking us to spiritual, emotional, and psychological maturity. He's leading us by His hands and taking us through the stages of maturation that require us to evolve and become more unified with His nature.

As humans and spiritual beings, we are living organisms. If we are not constantly changing and developing, we are decaying. Obtaining healing and freedom from what holds us captive is part of the process of growth and wholeness.

Everything that God touches grows. It's impossible for you to walk with God and not grow or produce. At some point in your walk with God, He is going to orchestrate and bring about change. Most of the time God will intentionally make us uncomfortable so we can grow and mature. Sometimes, God will allow us to get frustrated in certain areas of our lives so that our frustration can be used as the catalyst to bring about the change that God is birthing in us. God is constantly developing us through every stage of life and through the processes that we go through.

There is a saying that I love, *"Change only happens when the pain of staying the same is greater than the pain of change."* Basically, when you are sick and tired of staying the same, you are forced to grow.

"And all of us, as with unveiled face, [because we] continued to behold [in the Word of God] as in a mirror the glory of the Lord, are constantly being transfigured into His very own image in ever increasing splendor and from one degree of glory to another; [for this comes] from the Lord [Who is] the Spirit." 2 Corinthians 3:18 (AMPC)

It's time for us to embrace change that produces growth, so we can evolve and progressively become whole.

At times, our lives are disrupted by pain or by the evil injustices of life. We've all heard the saying that, *"bad things happen to good people."* There are some circumstances that we've experienced that brought sorrow and tragedies, and as a result, distorted our perception of God's love. Let's be clear: God is not the author of the evil that we've gone through. God has given us free will to choose good or evil. We live in a fallen world, with people who, unfortunately, have chosen the path of destruction. Some of us have been preys and victims at the hands of bad actors and people with evil intentions. I believe that God uses all of our experiences in life - the good, the bad, and the ugly ones - to heal us, grow us, and redeem our lives for His glory. Many of us have been damaged and mishandled through life's journey, but God's redemptive work is growing us to a state of wholeness.

Wholeness is a transformative healing process that is essential to our spiritual maturity.

As we grow in wholeness, we are faced with the realities of our brokenness, wounds, and emotional instability. That's when God invites us to trust Him deeper with our pain and disappointment as He begins the process of maturity.

Our spiritual maturity is very similar to a child's development. It takes the right nutrients for a baby to grow and become a child. In the same way, God expects us to grow up from childhood to adulthood with the spiritual nourishment of the Word of God. God is calling us to maturity, and it starts by giving Him access to the broken and damaged areas of our lives. As we yield to God's healing hands, we will be thrust into uncomfortable places that will produce in us the fruit of righteousness and truth.

Wholeness can't happen if the truth of God's word doesn't permeate the soil of our hearts. Becoming whole and evolving into the son or daughter God called us to be, will demand that we unlearn unhealthy mindsets we picked up on our journey. There are some perspectives we develop over time as a result of the trauma some of us experienced in life. On their journey to wholeness, some people will have to confront their inability to be decisive because of an insecurity to trust their own judgment. Others have been plagued with self-doubt since they were in their teens due to the unhealthy belief that they are not good enough.

Part of becoming whole is submitting to the changing power of the Word of God. Our mind, our will, and emotions, which essentially comprise our soul, can only be altered over time as we become doers of the Word. The nature of the Word of God is such that it has the capacity to take us through a spiritual, mental, and psychological metamorphosis when applied diligently.

James 1:22 encourages us to put into practice the truths found in the Bible.

> *"But don't just listen to God's word. You must do what it says. Otherwise, you are only fooling yourselves." James 1:22 (NLT)*

By doing what the word of God says, we begin to shed mindsets and thinking patterns that are often limiting or destructive. That's when we begin to grow and fully develop. Spiritual maturity happens when we become doers of the Word of God and not just hearers.

It's in practicing the Word of God that our spiritual maturity is forged. God is requiring more from each of us because He is always calling us to go deeper. In order for us to mature, we need to fall in love with the Word of God and apply it to our daily lives. The Word of God is the only tool that can transform us into the likeness of Jesus Christ.

The Word of God uncovers our spiritual condition and heals our soul. Hebrews 4:12 reminds us that:

> "the Word that God speaks is alive and full of power [making it active, operative, energizing, and effective]; it is sharper than any two-edged sword, penetrating to the dividing line of the [breath of life (soul) and [the immortal] spirit, and of joints and marrow [of the deepest parts of our nature], exposing and sifting and analyzing and judging the very thoughts and purposes of the heart." (AMPC)

What is the evidence that we're growing and becoming whole? The evidence that we are growing in Christ lies in the fruits that we bear. Can others witness the effects that the Word of God is producing in us? Have we fully embraced the healing that God's Word provides? What do our actions and patterns reveal about the condition of our hearts? Does our walk with God demonstrate a high level of integrity? Can people recognize that we are followers of Christ by the love and compassion we have for others?

Jesus says in John 15:8:

> "When you bear (produce) much fruit, My Father is honored and glorified, and you show and prove yourselves to be true followers of Mine." (AMPC)

Applying the truth of the Word of God in our life, is proven to make us whole, but also provides opportunities for God to be glorified.

I believe that God is calling us into a deeper pursuit of truth as we're on this spiritual growth journey. I believe that there is always more of God available for each of us. We determine how much of God we truly desire in our lives.

> "When you come looking for Me, you'll find Me. Yes, when you get serious about finding Me and want it more than anything else, I'll make sure you won't be disappointed... I'll turn things around for you." Jeremiah 29:13-14 (MSG)

Our spiritual growth is vital to the success of our lives. If we don't invest in our spiritual maturity, we are robbing ourselves (and we are robbing the body of Christ) of the potential to become the mature son or daughter God called us to be. I truly believe that it's God's desire to grow us to a state of harmony with Christ. As the world looks at us, they should see a reflection of Christ's character and image.

Below are areas of our lives that give us an indication of whether or not we're growing and becoming whole.

1. The way we treat people.

Do we treat people with dignity and respect? Is the love of God evident in the way we address each other? The way we treat people who have lower economic status than we do tells a lot about our character. Do we favor people who have material wealth over those who can do nothing for us?

> "By this shall all [men] know that you are My disciples, if you love one another [if you keep on showing love among yourselves]." John 13:35 (AMPC)

> "Love one another with brotherly affection [as members of one family], giving precedence and showing honor to one another." Romans 12:10 (AMPC)

2. The way we handle adversity and tests.

What is our attitude when we are going through the fire? Do we understand that the testing of our faith produces perseverance or are we like the children of Israel who constantly complain in hard times?

> "Consider it wholly joyful, my brethren, whenever you are enveloped in or encounter trials of any sort or fall into various temptations. Be assured and understand that the trial and proving of your faith bring out endurance and steadfastness and patience. But let endurance and steadfastness and patience have full play and do a thorough work, so

that you may be [people] perfectly and fully developed [with no defects], lacking in nothing." James 1:2-4 (AMPC)

3. The way we handle offenses.

The Bible guarantees that we are going to be offended in life. It's inevitable. Someone at work is going to say something that upsets you or will treat you in a condescending manner. Even your family and friends will sometimes offend you, but our response to that offense determines whether we are maturing or not. Are we quick to extend forgiveness or do we get in our feelings and retaliate?

"He who covers and forgives an offense seeks love, but he who repeats or harps on a matter separates even close friends." Proverbs 17:9 (AMPC)

"You shall not take revenge or bear any grudge against the sons of your people, but you shall love your neighbor as yourself. I am the Lord." Leviticus 19:18 (AMPC)

4. The way we handle blessings.

Do we become puffed up when God blesses us, or do we remain humble? Some folks completely change when God blesses them financially. You won't even recognize them anymore. They toss all humility out the door and adopt a prideful attitude. This reveals the crack of selfish ambition and pride that was present in their hearts the whole time. Wealth and prestige have a way of revealing who people really are.

"What are you so puffed up about? What do you have that God hasn't given you? And if all you have is from God, why act as though you are so great, and as though you have accomplished something on your own?" 1 Corinthians 4:7 (The Living Bible)

5. What we value in life.

What we value or neglect can give us an indication of the areas of growth we need to focus on. Do we put high importance on living right before God and staying in His Word? Do we value a lifestyle based on integrity? Are we good stewards over the relationships that God has given us? Or have we gotten too familiar with people that we no longer honor their presence?

Thriving From A Place Of Rest

If we're honest with ourselves, life can be very stressful at times. The reality is that we live in a chaotic and fallen world. If you're a person who naturally stays out of trouble and out of people's business, somehow trouble can still find you. Isn't that the truth? Things are not always perfect, not always the way that we want them to be. Sometimes we encounter difficulties at work, or we have to resolve conflicts in our family relationships. The truth is, it's not always easy to navigate through life's circumstances.

There's always a storm or a challenging situation waiting around the corner. At times, when you've done everything you know to do, the best thing you can do is to learn to rest in God. I've come to understand that the posture of resting in God and quieting the soul is the best way to fully grow in our ability to trust God. I believe you can experience inner peace in the midst of a raging storm. As we continue to mature in God, we learn to praise Him through the pain, the tears, the frustrations, the rejections, and the disappointments. That's when we learn that only God can provide what we need. The answer and the breakthrough you're looking for can only come from Him. Anchor your heart, your emotions, and your mind in Christ. On Christ, the solid rock we stand, and all other ground is sinking sand. When you've done all else, keep standing. It's in Him that we find our rest. Our ability to find rest in God is also deeply connected to the process of becoming whole. The more we grow in wholeness, the more secure we become and the more we make decisions from a place of rest.

> *"For thus said the Lord God, the Holy One of Israel: In returning [to Me] and resting [in Me] you shall be saved; in quietness and in [trusting] confidence shall be your strength." Isaiah 30:15 (AMPC)*

If God himself created the world in six days and then rested on the seventh day, what makes you think that you can thrive in life with no rest? God doesn't get tired nor needs sleep, so the reason He rested after creation was to highlight the importance of finding the rest our souls need.

Hebrews 4:1-11 discusses the rest that God has promised to everyone who believes in Him:

> *"God's promise of entering his rest still stands, so we ought to tremble with fear that some of you might fail to experience it. For this good news—that God has prepared this rest—has been announced to us just as it was to them. But it did them no good because they didn't share the faith of those who listened to God. For only we who believe can enter his rest. As for the others, God said, 'In my anger, I took an oath:*
>
> *'They will never enter my place of rest,' even though this rest has been ready since he made the world. We know it is ready because of the place in the Scriptures where it mentions the seventh day, 'On the seventh day God rested from all his work.' But in the other passage God said, 'They will never enter my place of rest.'*
>
> *God's rest is there for people to enter, but those who first heard this good news failed to enter because they disobeyed God. So God set another time for entering his rest, and that time is today. God announced this through David much later in the words already quoted, 'Today when you hear his voice, don't harden your hearts.'*
>
> *Now, if Joshua had succeeded in giving them this rest, God would not have spoken about another day of rest still to come. **"So there is a special rest still waiting for the people of God. For all who have entered into God's rest have rested from their labors, just as God did after***

creating the world. So let us do our best to enter that rest. But if
we disobey God, as the people of Israel did, we will fall." (NLT)

We understand from the passage of Scripture we just read, that our ability to rest in God is predicated on our faith and willingness to obey Him. As we've stated in previous chapters, our obedience to God is directly indicative of our spiritual maturity. When we enter into God's rest, we're no longer striving in our own strength or grinding to make things happen according to our timetable. Resting in God is an aspect of walking in wholeness and finding contentment in who God is.

The chaos of the world that takes place externally can no longer affect your internal core when we find stability and security in God's rest. When you're grounded in Christ and completely rooted in who He is, the external things no longer affect you negatively.

We live in a society that glorifies stress and the idea of being busy. Especially around the holidays, many people feel overwhelmed and overworked. We try to meet society's expectations and drive ourselves crazy in our attempt to meet people's needs. It can be extremely exhausting for our souls. I'm convinced that God didn't call us to be busy. He called us to be fruitful.

What Does It Mean To Live From A Place Of Rest?

When Christ is the air you breathe, you can find rest for your soul. You're only going to be efficient in life when you operate from a place of rest. A lot of people are not even aware that their soul and body are bankrupt because they're completely burned out. The abundant life that Jesus promised in John 10:10, is available to each of us when we enter and abide in that place of rest. Outside of Christ, life will never be meaningful or satisfying. I believe that God wants us to live from a place of overflow, but many people live life depleted, with their tanks always empty. You can't give what you don't have, so make sure your spirit, soul, and body are properly nurtured and fed, so you can operate at your highest potential.

1. Prioritizing God's Will.

First thing first, living life from a place of rest means that we've got to be aligned with God's perfect will. Matthew 6:33 (My paraphrase) reminds us to seek the Kingdom of God above everything else and live righteously, then God will supply everything else we need. Living from a place of rest also means relinquishing control of the way you think your life should be and embracing God's will for your life. Our dreams need to be aligned with God's plans for our lives. When there's an internal tug of war between your will and God's will for your life, there's often a lack of peace present in your heart. Living a harmonious lifestyle will only happen when your life is in sync with God's will.

2. Trusting God and His Timing.

When we rest in God, we are given the opportunity to grow in all aspects of trust. Trusting in God's sovereignty means that we recognize His preeminence above all things, and we submit to the ways He's executing His plan. When we have that understanding, we have a full assurance that God is responsible for us. As a loving Father, He's responsible to provide for us, to protect us, and to give us identity, which are the basic necessities we need to maximize our potential in life. With that in mind, we can trust that in His sovereignty, He knows exactly what's best for us.

God knows the things that matter to you. He's well aware of the desires of your heart, but the reality is that God is not in a hurry. The problem is us; we're always operating from a place of emergency. Everything must happen overnight because we live in a microwave mentality of society. If we learn to prioritize what matters to God, He will take care of what we care about the most. Trusting God and His timing, also means that we've got to give God room to orchestrate the outcomes that glorify Him. That's real trust.

3. Cultivating a Thriving Soul.

Living from a place of rest, also means that we need to protect the health of our soul. The same way we're aware that we have to eat healthily and take care of our physical bodies, we also have a responsibility to care for our souls.

We decide what we expose our minds to. Our souls are a fertile soil that will reproduce fruits from the seeds we plant. It's up to us to plant seeds that will continue to foster a thriving soul.

Additionally, it's important that we learn to protect our mental space by setting proper boundaries. There are some relationships that are toxic to your mental and spiritual health. Learn to either cut those relationships or love them from a distance. If someone is always reminding you of your past, of who you used to be, you should keep them in your past and move on with your life. Anyone who doesn't want you to evolve and grow needs to stay behind.

Growing in wholeness is a result of living life in harmony with the presence of God. It's a process of truly becoming one with the Father as we're molded by His Holy Spirit. When our spiritual, mental, and emotional well-being is aligned with who God is, we can fully experience the abundant life that is available to all believers.

Prophetic Declaration

Dear Resilient Soul

He who lives in you is greater than the pressure and weight of the external world. Christ is your anchor and the solid rock that sustains your life. When you know the Prince of Peace and allow Him to cultivate an atmosphere of inner peace in your heart and mind, you can thrive and be successful regardless of the challenges and external circumstances. The chaos of life can't shake a person whose roots are deeply grounded in God's unfailing love.

When your spirit is eternally intertwined with the Holy Spirit, nothing can break you. We can withstand any situation life throws at us, because His strength is made perfect in our weakness. When God is your oxygen, the world cannot suffocate you. Rise up resilient one, and stand strong in God's might.

From your mother's womb, God has chosen you and appointed you as His prophet to the nations. Speak His word and perform that which you are called to do. You will one day give an account of how you used your gifts, time, and resources.

The Great I Am, the Alpha, and the Omega, is already in your future. No need to fear what tomorrow brings. Know that your breakthroughs are helping others break free from their own chains. You may never know who is inspired by your resilience and strength. While you are overcoming your own challenges, people are finding courage through your journey. Our victories are not just for ourselves, they are also for the benefit of others.

Persist until you succeed, so you can inspire generations to come.

8

Love Liberates

"I'm grateful to have been loved and to be loved now and to be able to love, because that liberates. Love liberates. It doesn't just hold - that's ego. Love liberates. It doesn't bind."
—Dr. Maya Angelou

We've all experienced a level of distress and pain, but some of us have never found the courage to reveal those scars to the world. The fear of being judged or being perceived as less than, often hinders us from being utterly vulnerable. The truth is, our vulnerability is, at times, the catalyst that accelerates our healing and propels us to our freedom. Our painful experiences were never meant to be hidden. We've got to find the strength within us to remove our masks and uncover our scars, so others can partake in that same healing power. Sharing is caring. Sharing is touching souls. Sharing is empowering others to find their own voices.

I believe that our journeys are intertwined and woven together by the Master's fingerprints. The thread of His love intricately stitches our humanity into a beautiful tapestry. It's only the love of God that can penetrate the fiber of our being and heal our wounds. The unfailing love of God empowers us to forgive even when we hurt the most. Extending forgiveness to others is the greatest love testament of God's love working within us.

Forgiveness is not an easy choice to embrace. It doesn't condone the bad behavior, nor does it erase the hurtful memories. Forgiveness does something greater. It frees our hearts from bitterness and revenge, so we can learn to love as God does. On my journey, I've come to realize that forgiveness doesn't just happen instantaneously. It happens in layers, similar to peeling an onion.

When you decide to forgive someone who has deeply wounded you, you will find yourself having to choose to let go daily. The key is to slowly let go of the pain suffocating your heart, so that you can freely receive God's healing power. When those painful memories resurface, take a deep breath, and choose to let go. It's a daily choice. To forgive others is to set yourself free.

I truly believe that God never wastes an experience. Though He is not the originator of our pain and sorrow, He redeems all we've gone through for a greater purpose. I used to be ashamed of my wounds and failures. For too long, I was emotionally numb, unable to express the agony that was afflicting my soul. I would suppress my feelings because it was the only coping mechanism I had to avoid confronting the destructive thoughts I had about myself. I didn't know how to love myself, and frankly, I didn't think I was worthy of love.

It's easier to love yourself when you're polished, or when you feel accomplished in a certain area. It's easier to love others when they are on their best behaviors. But can we truly love ourselves when we fail, when we stumble, or when we realize that our character still needs refining? When we look at ourselves in the mirror, do we nitpick every imperfection?

"Whoever does not love does not know God, because God is love." 1 John 4:8

God loves you with the total sums of all your imperfections and wounds. Your scars do not diminish your value in His sight. No matter what you've gone through, your worth in God's eyes will never be tarnished. God loves you with an everlasting love. A love that passionately pursues us and covers our shame. God demonstrated His perfect love for us by sending His only son to bear the penalty of our sins (Romans 5:8). We are worth every nail that pierced Jesus' hands to the cross.

I believe that we are unable to experience the depth of the love of God without being intimately acquainted with God himself. Our freedom to love can only originate from Him, simply because He represents the very essence of love. God's love first encountered me and broke the chains that were preventing me from loving myself. When I learned to love myself despite my imperfections, I stopped comparing myself to others, and I genuinely began to love others as God does.

The greatest power in the Universe is the Love of God. The Bible tells us, as we know, in John 3:16 that God so loved the world that He gave his only begotten son that whoever believes in Him will not perish but have everlasting life. It was the love of God that propelled Jesus to the cross even when He clearly knew that we had the choice to either choose Him or reject Him.

Let's look at specific attributes of the love of God:

The Love Of God Uncovers Our Identity

There are so many Christians in the Body of Christ struggling with identity issues, because they haven't experienced the tangible manifestation of the love of God. Many today are victims of spiritual identity theft, because the enemy has placed a veil over their hearts hindering them from understanding their position in Christ. I believe that the love of God is a transformative agent that reveals our true identity and worth in Christ Jesus. Satan doesn't want us to believe that we're more than conquerors and that we've been chosen by God to rule and reign as co-heirs with Christ. When we come to the realization that we were bought with the highest price, we will no longer allow the world to diminish our value. Our ability to influence the culture hinges on our understanding of sonship/daughtership. And it's the love of God that unlocks the revelation that we were designed in the image of God, with the fullness of His attributes and qualities.

The love of God is also the cure to every ailment that plagues the church and our culture. For the love of God to deliver us and set us free, we need to acknowledge our deep need for God. If we are comfortable in our sins and everything else that is ungodly that the church hides behind closed doors, we cannot be transformed by the love of The Father. Only when we acknowledge our brokenness and dependence on God that He can fill us with His love. We need to recognize that we desperately need God's loving presence in our lives. Many Christians today are not walking in wholeness in their souls, because they haven't allowed the love of God to confront the pain, the emotional baggage, hurtful memories, and fears that are keeping their souls in bondage.

I'm here to tell you that the greatest force in the universe is still the love of God. Only the love of God can melt your heart of stone and cause repentance to flow from it. The love of God changes you. One encounter with the Father's heart will transform you and leave you thirsting for more of God. The love of God changes our sinful cravings and transforms us into true sons and daughters of God. I believe that the longing of God's heart is for each of us to understand the gift of sonship/daughtership. The Spirit of sonship is released when we fully receive the love of God in our hearts. When we understand that the Creator of the Universe is our Abba Father, our identity becomes sealed in Christ Jesus.

"For as many as are led by the Spirit of God, these are sons of God. For you did not receive the spirit of bondage again to fear, but you received the Spirit of adoption (Spirit of Sonship) by whom we cry out, "Abba, Father." The Spirit Himself bears witness with our spirit that we are children of God, and if children, then heirs—heirs of God and joint heirs with Christ, if indeed we suffer with Him, that we may also be glorified together." Romans 8:15-17

The Love Of God Confronts Our Disobedience

The Love of God is the very nature of God; it's the essence of who He is. When people say, *"God is Love"* (1 John 4:8), I don't think they fully understand the depth of that scripture. Some use that scripture "God is Love" to excuse their behavior as if it gives them a license to continue to sin. In some people's mind, it's synonymous with "don't judge me," because God is love.

I'm here to remind us that the Love of God will also correct us when we stray away from God's Word and His will. The Bible clearly says that God chastises whom He loves. When you are a legitimate son or daughter of the living God, you will be corrected, because He loves you enough that He desires that you remain on the narrow path.

> *"My son (and daughter), do not make light of the Lord's discipline, and do not lose heart when He rebukes you, because the Lord disciplines the one he loves, and He chastens everyone He accepts as His son (and daughter)."*
> *Hebrews 12:6 (NIV)*

God loves us so much that His goal is to transform us into the likeness of His Son Jesus Christ. God doesn't leave you in the same sinful garment that you came to Him with, He transforms your heart and your mind if you allow His Love to penetrate your life.

The Love Of God Empowers Us To Forgive

The love of God teaches us to forgive. Everyone has the capacity to grow in the area of forgiveness, if we're willing. I believe that the Holy Spirit working within us, gives us the grace to forgive those who misused and abused us. As mentioned earlier, forgiveness is a daily choice. The Holy Spirit helps us process the painful situation, but the decision to let go of the pain is ours. We decide if we will continue to be bitter, angry, or if we will use the painful situation to be better. In Matthew 18:21 when Peter asked Jesus how many times he should forgive others, Jesus replied and said, *"77 times."* In essence, Jesus said that we should put the love of God on display at all times and forgive others every opportunity we get.

> *"Love does not dishonor others, it is not self-seeking, it is not easily angered, it keeps no record of wrongs. Love does not delight in evil but rejoices with the truth." 1 Corinthians 13:5-6 (NIV)*

Allow the love of God to permeate your heart today; God wants to minister to each of us today and transform us. Whatever baggage or disappointment you're carrying, I would like to encourage you to exchange that for the love of God. Give God access to your heart; give Him access to those areas of your heart that you are ashamed of. God wants to heal His sons and daughters and break every cycle holding us captive. The love of God breaks every chain, limitation, and glass ceiling. The freedom we've been longing for, can only be released when we allow the Holy Spirit to perfect God's love in our souls.

The love of God never fails, never gives up on us, and never runs out. It's the only force that will satisfy our souls because nothing else will. God wants to encounter us and transform us by His love.

The love of God protects us against spiritual blind spots. When we're blinded, we can't see. I've found that the love of God often protects us from making bad decisions. The love of God has a way of redirecting our steps and closing the doors that we're not meant to walk in. Sometimes when things don't go our way, we feel as if we've been rejected. You weren't rejected; you were redirected because of God's love. God loves us too much to see us go down paths that are not beneficial to us. Often, we don't have enough discernment to identify if a path is God's choice for us. That's when the love of God steps in and reveals God's pathway for us. Trust God's ability to love you. He knows exactly what's best for you according to His divine blueprint.

The Love Of God Delivers Us From Fear

God's love delivers us from one of Satan's common weapons of destruction, fear. Let's be clear that fear is a spirit. It's a technique that the enemy uses to blind our spiritual eyes and distort our realities. Fear cripples and hinders us from boldly walking in the direction of God's path for us. It often causes us to shrink in the face of adversity or problems.

Let's dive into the Scriptures and understand the agenda behind the spirit of fear.

2 Kings 6:8-23 highlights the Arameans plot to kill the Prophet Elisha. In those days, The Lord was using the Prophet Elisha to provide direction and counsel to the King of Israel. The King of Aram, the enemy of the Israelites, did not appreciate the fact that God would reveal to the Prophet Elisha the plans He had to invade Israel. In verse 12, King Aram's servant told him, *"Elisha, the prophet who is in Israel, tells the king of Israel the words that you speak in your bedroom."* The King of Aram decided to plot an agenda to capture Elisha, so he sent chariots and horses to invade the city of Dothan where Elisha resided.

Elisha's servant got up early to realize that their enemies had encircled them. Elisha's servant was distraught and fearful. He said to him, *"Oh no, my master! What are we to do?"* Elisha answered:

> *"Do not be afraid, for those who are with us are more than those who are with them."* Then Elisha prayed and said, *"Lord, please, open his eyes that he may see."* And the Lord opened the servants eyes and he saw; and behold, the mountain was full of horses and chariots of fire surrounding Elisha. When the Arameans came down to him, Elisha prayed to the Lord and said, *"Please strike this people (nation) with]blindness."* And God struck them with blindness, in accordance with Elisha's request. Then Elisha said to the Arameans, *"This is not the way, nor is this the city. Follow me and I will lead you to the man whom you are seeking."* And he led them to Samaria." *2 Kings 6:15-19 (AMP)*

Have you ever noticed when kids are afraid, they close their eyes? They cover their sight, which hinders their ability to actually see. I've realized that fear is often the weapon of choice of the enemy because it has the ability to incapacitate and immobilize its prey. Fear distorts your vision and creates a false reality of the situation you're facing. The danger is when your brain starts believing in the distorted reality that fear promotes. At that moment, your ability to see the situation through the eyes of faith is compromised. I truly believe that fear is an attack on our faith. Your spiritual eyes are the lens of faith. When our faith is under attack, our ability to believe God is limited. Fear hinders our faith from fully maturing.

In the passage above, Elisha's servant was clearly fearful of the chariots and horses that were aiming to attack them. He was focused on his natural sight and couldn't see God's provision in the spiritual realm. How often do we fixate our natural sight on negative things and fail to ask God to open our spiritual eyes to the things He's doing in our lives? Fear represents an attack of the enemy on your ability to see with the eyes of the Spirit.

When we are faced with fear, there are only two responses that we can have. We can either be overwhelmed by the fear and allow fear to intimidate us. Or, we can decide to rise up in our God-given identity as spiritual sons and daughters and confront that spirit of fear. Fear is a bully. Its agenda is to silence our voices and cause us to relinquish our position in Christ. Fear gives you the illusion that it controls your thoughts and actions. However, know that bullies are insecure and are often intimidated by our great potential. Fear's biggest threat is a believer, who is completely sold out to the cause of Christ and fully operates in God's love.

There are three types of fear that most people deal with, that I would like to highlight in the section below:

Fear Of Failure

I've met some people who won't even try new experiences or make any life-changing decisions because of the fear of failure. They automatically disqualify themselves from the opportunities awaiting them on the other side of their fear. That fear of failure robs them of the impact they are destined to make in the lives of so many people. Once people fail, they label themselves as failures and refuse to try again. Understand that failure is an event. It's certainly not your identity.

Failure is part of the journey of life. All of us have failed in one way or another, whether it was in school, in our professional careers, or even in the area of relationships. Failure can be one of the best teachers life kindly gives us. In order for us to grow, learn, and develop our character, we need to understand the value of failure. When we fully receive the liberty that comes from the love of God, we will have a different perspective of failure. Being fully secure in our identity as sons and daughters of God, we then understand that our value is not diminished by the failures we experience in life.

Fear Of Rejection

Rejection is also an aspect of life that many of us have faced at some point on our journey. The fear of rejection stems from our desire as human beings to belong, be seen, heard, and understood. When one of these areas isn't met, we often feel invisible, unwanted, undervalued, and can often experience a sense of deep hurt. The fear of rejection keeps us from taking chances and expressing our feelings or standing up for ourselves. The same fear intimidates us from asking for that pay raise, from championing new ideas, or from starting that new business venture.

Do not let rejection influence your self-worth. Jesus thought you were worth dying for. You are fully loved by a God who thinks you are the most beautiful creature He created. Even when others do not recognize your worth or don't place value on what you offer, know that you matter simply because God says so. Face that fear head-on and become your own life coach. Only speak positive words over your life, that build and encourage you to rise above that fear. Remember that negative self-talk is destructive and can easily become self-fulfilling prophecies.

Fear Of Success

In life, success often yields greater responsibility. A promotion is often an invitation for additional duties and commitments. Experiencing success in any field will cost you great sacrifice, time, and sweat equity. I believe that we all have to be ready mentally, emotionally, and spiritually to face the consequences that success brings. We should all aspire to live a successful life. And let's be clear, success is a very subjective concept. It's highly influenced by your own desires and by what you want out of life. Regardless of what that picture looks like for you, I believe that God wants us to live successful and fulfilled lives.

However, sometimes people aren't able to handle the pressures that come with success. For some, the fear of standing out and being a subject matter expert in their field is an uncomfortable position. The pressure and responsibility of success will cause some to, therefore, sabotage their own progress. Fear of success can also manifest in someone's constant urge to procrastinate or to avoid setting higher goals. Fear of not being qualified, smart, or worthy enough to handle success overwhelms them from stepping into all that God has called them to do.

Are You Challenged By Fear Or Overwhelmed By It?

Remind yourself of your identity in Christ and meditate on who God calls you. Your validation and approval come from God. He is the only one who can define you, for He knows who you are and what you carry. He intricately formed you in your mother's womb, so God is deeply acquainted with you.

Believe in the vision that is burning in your heart. Believe in the idea that the Lord has laid on your heart. Understand that you are no longer a slave to fear, but you are God's child. One way to overcome fear is to understand who you are and whose you are. You are a child of the Most High God and you've been endowed with great skills, abilities, and a great calling. You have an assignment to add value to the people that you are called to serve.

The love of God has made provisions for our shortcomings, pain, and struggles. There is absolutely nothing we can do that can deter God's love from pursuing us. Love is the very essence of God's nature. It's a powerfully transformative agent that breaks the shackles of our souls and allows us to fully come alive as sons and daughters of God. Love gives us permission to unapologetically walk in the freedom that Christ has already purchased.

> "And as we live in God, our love grows more perfect. So we will not be afraid on the day of judgment, but we can face him with confidence because we live like Jesus here in this world. Such love has no fear, because perfect love expels all fear. If we are afraid, it is for fear of punishment, and this shows that we have not fully experienced his perfect love." 1 John 4:17-18 (NLT)

I believe that the Holy Spirit in us is growing and cultivating the love of God in our hearts to full maturity. As we fully yield to the wisdom and workings of the Holy Spirit, we will find security and safety in God's perfect love. We will no longer be tossed to and fro by the spirit of rejection, fear, or intimidation. Because we've been touched by the love of God, we have full liberty to reign and rule as mature sons and daughters of God.

Conclusion

As a son or daughter of the Most High God, you were born into the Kingdom of God for such a time as this. Your presence on this earth is strategic and very intentional. So many people's breakthroughs are dependent on your willingness to obey God and to urgently do all that He has already placed in your heart. The enemy of your soul, the devil, is greatly intimidated by your resilience and determination to follow Christ till the end. He tried to slow you down and derail your purpose; however, his plans were to no avail. You were so deeply rooted and hidden in Christ, that he is unable to disrupt your thoughts, your actions, and the trajectory of your life.

This is the time to fully awaken to the greatness of your calling. Realize that time is of the essence. Now is the time to act. Your future children and grandchildren will one day read about the exploits that you were bold enough to pursue. You are called to be bold and to stand up against mindsets and limiting belief systems that are contrary to God's ways. There's greater power on the inside of you to resist the lies that the culture promotes. There is no glass ceiling that can withstand the anointing of God upon your life. You are God's vessel. You are His weapon of choice against the schemes of Satan.

That vision, that's been burning in your heart, is crying out for expression. Bring it to fruition. Fully step into the field that God has called you to influence. Own that territory. It's yours for the taking. Now is the time to position yourself to overtake the enemies that have been intimidating your family for decades. You've been assigned to change the narrative. You will do everything that your parents and grandparents weren't able to accomplish. Never forget that you've been embraced by the Father's love. You've been chosen as one of the leaders called to represent Him in our culture. You are the head and not the tail, above and not beneath. You are not a second-class citizen. You're God's ambassador, handpicked to carry His mission to the Nations of the world.

God knows what He is doing, and a day will come when your past and present will make sense. In the waiting, we have to lean on His strength. It's not easy, but I don't know about you, I'd rather remain in the center of God's perfect will for my life. I don't want to birth an Ishmael by trying to "help" God and do things my own way; I will wait on my promise, Isaac. I pray today for every soldier who's been waiting for the promises of God to manifest. May you find the strength to persevere through the waiting season. May God wrap you in His arms of LOVE today, in Jesus' name.

> *"Let us not become weary in doing good, for at the proper time we will reap a harvest if we do not give up." Galatians 6:9*

We serve a limitless God. Infinite. All-powerful. All-knowing. All-capable. There is nothing too hard for Him. Anchor your heart, your mind, and your emotions in His unfailing nature. God cannot fail. He cannot lie. He cannot disappoint. He is a great Father. Challenge your doubts today with the Word of God! Expect miracles, signs, and wonders to follow you all the days of your life!

I only have one burning desire and that's to please God and live a purposeful life. At the end of my journey, I long to hear those words, *"Well done, my good and faithful servant."* I will go through the fire, the valley, and the storms of life just to hear those words. My life is not my own. It's an amazing joy to know God intimately.

I desire that each of us fully embrace our identity as sons and daughters of the living God. Nothing in life is meaningful if we don't first prioritize our relationship and friendship with God. Your Heavenly Father wants you to know that:

Your dreams are significant.

Your presence is significant.

Your existence is significant.

Your voice is significant.

Your sacrifices are significant.

Your journey is significant.

Your tears are significant.

Your fingerprint is significant.

Your purpose is significant.

YOU ARE SIGNIFICANT.

You belong to God our Father, and you have an amazing purpose. He sees you, and He knows you by name. May you never feel invisible or inadequate ever again.

You're not just occupying space on the earth; you are destined to be here, in this generation, to glorify the Father, solve specific problems, and leave a lasting LEGACY.

You are God's chosen vessel. Live the life that God created you for.

Arise, son and daughter of the Living God!

Notes

INTRODUCTION

1   U.S. Census Bureau, Current Population Survey, "Living Arrangements of Children under 18 Years/1 and Marital Status of Parents by Age, Sex, Race, and Hispanic Origin/2 and Selected Characteristics of the Child for all Children 2010." Table C3. Internet Release Date November, 2010.

2   U.S. Census Bureau, Current Population Survey, "Living Arrangements of Children under 18 Years/1 and Marital Status of Parents by Age, Sex, Race, and Hispanic Origin/2 and Selected Characteristics of the Child for all Children 2010." Table C3. Internet Release Date November, 2010.

NO LONGER AN ORPHAN

3   Translated as "the right time" from Ancient Greek, kairos variously refers to an "opportune presentation" in rhetoric and a "spiritual opportunity" in Christian theology.

4   Relational Intelligence by Dr. Dharius Daniels, "rejection infection" on page 154-155.

5   The Armor of God by Priscilla Shirer, Strengthen Your Core on page 43.

THE BRIDE PRICE

6   Report on People, Pornography & Age Verification (bbfc, January 2020) https://www.revealingreality.co.uk/wp-content/uploads/2020/01/BBFC-Young-people-and-pornography-Final-report-2401.pdf

IDENTITY OF TRUE SONS & DAUGHTERS

7   American Psychology Association, APA Dictionary of Psychology, Definition of Identity. https://dictionary.apa.org/identity

8   National Geographic, Resource Library Article, "Women of NASA". https://bit.ly/376Sg8e

CREATED FOR INTIMACY

9   The Elijah List, Article by James W. Goll (God Encounters Ministries), "Holy Spirit, You are welcome here." http://www.elijahlist.com/words/display_word.html?ID=24983

About the Author

Dumbi Mabiala is a certified speaker and passionate mentor whose voice of wisdom has influenced many around the globe. She's the Founder of Mentoring Generations, an organization with the mandate to develop leaders in ministry and in the marketplace through spiritual mentorship and leadership. She's had the pleasure over the years to speak to various audiences at seminars, women's conferences, retreats and local organizations events. Her authenticity and innate ability to relate to people of all walks of life, cultural backgrounds and upbringings are just some of the qualities that are easily seen through her teachings. She has the heart of a mentor as she empowers generations to effectively fulfill their God given calling.

You can connect with me on:

🌐 https://dumbimabiala.org